# ANGEL

NEESHANT SRIVASTAVA

Made with ♥ on the Notion Press Platform
www.notionpress.com

Dedicated to the two people I love the most. My dear Papa and Mummy.

# Contents

# A VILLAGE IN JALANDHAR

ANGEL

• 2 •

A VILLAGE OF COURAGE

The year was 1984, the busiest year of a nation trying find its place in the world. It was a year of great tragedy, a black year in the history of India. Generations after, people have not forgotten that year completely, and perhaps never will.

Sq. Ldr. Nakul Dev was transferred to Jalandhar as the next in a series of postings. Some technical problems and Nakul could not find a place in the Air Force Station, Adampur. He was sent to a village deep in oblivion in remote Jalandhar. Nakul tried his best to find a place in the Air Force station, but in vain. With a heavy heart he travelled on a truck with his family of two younger sons and a wife named Radha. His belongings had been curtailed for he got rid of a lot of belongings during the transfer. Nakul knew what was going on in the nation, but Radha and the kids were totally ignorant. Children just felt the breeze and the never-ending fields of grain and other crops along the way. Nature always stayed aloof to what happened in the family of humans and each flower dressed up the paradise. The air spoke of happiness and the sunshine had a greater glow than gold. Humans just know the language of distress and feel worse than animals do. Beauty vanishes the moment hatred fills the heart. Nakul knew all of that and sometimes wanted to see the world through his children's eyes. The simplest thing that God created is love, and it is the hardest thing to do in the world. The truck often felt the jerks of an uneven road but the sweet weather compensated for it. The children's heads turned left and right periodically, as if they were missing something on each end. Nakul had a straight gaze, pensive, sad, like he had been punished for nothing. Radha was happy like always and sometimes uttered worlds of disbelief looking at the greenery around her. It was a long journey from the railway station to the village and the belongings at the back of the truck made a lot of noise, jumping and colliding with one another. Nakul felt he was growing old. Youth was far better when the mind was lighter and the load none to speak of. The days were spent in poetry and cigarettes. The motorbike was fun to ride and it took Nakul around the country on low fuel. Marriage changes every man and woman. Men often lose the wild streak of fun and woman act like trapped pigeons. The boys, Naresh and Suresh, ten and eight years old, saw a beautiful world just like in those Christmas songs. Naresh, the elder one, did not laugh much looking at the serious faces of his parents. Suresh was going berserk, like someone had poured some chilled ice water on him. A laugh was the lowest he got to and was often pulled down by his waist by the rough hands of Nakul. He just could not stay put. As a baby Suresh cried endlessly and brought Nakul into action. Radha was happy to see her baby go out of control and often let Suresh cry while she laughed.

The tired truck finally stopped and all the occupants were taken by surprise. They could hardly see the road in front of them because of the enormity of the truck. The first one to notice the sudden stop was Nakul. He looked at the worn-out driver and pushed the hard door of the truck. All members slowly got out, with great difficulty, especially the children and Radha in a sari. Nakul asked the driver to take a break from duty and get himself something to eat, while the family checked the house in the village. Suresh ran forward with speed, as if he was familiar with the house. Nakul stopped the boy urged him to hold his horses.

There was a narrow passage interspersed with walls of houses on either side. The grass grew in clumps on the baked mud floor without any design. Nakul bent down and read the house number of each house as he walked down the passage. They reached the end of the passage as it turned right into another passage. There was a pomegranate tree of the left side of a house that had tall boundary walls. Nakul bent low to check the number of the house and again and shook his head in affirmation,

'This is the one, kids.'

Suresh pushed the creaking wooden door and ran into a huge courtyard. The rooms were on the right as he saw a door in front of him. Before Nakul could say anything, he opened the door and ran in. To his surprise he saw a turban clad middle aged man sitting on a rocking chair.

'Who's that, my son?' the sardar was quick to ask.

Suresh was embarrassed and fearful. He just ran out of the door that he had entered by mistake as fast as he could. He ran to Radha and tried to hide behind her sari, like he often did in such a situation. Nakul inspected the house, the rooms, kitchen, the room on the first floor that also had a terrace, drawing room. Radha was more interested in the kitchen and did not take long to blend with it. A tall sardar walked into the courtyard and Nakul received him,

'Sorry to bother you sir, we are the new occupants of this house. I am Sq. Ldr. Nakul Dev with my family. We didn't know we had company. I guess this wired mesh door is the line that separates our two houses. We just arrived by train; our belongings are there in a truck. Did we bother you, sir.'

'Mr. Nakul we are so happy to have you here. We were waiting for you for quite some time. My name is Sukhwinder Singh. I have two sons, Joginder and Parminder and my dear wife Jassi. I apologize if I have caused any discomfort, just that we were not expecting you at this time. Feel free to get your belongings and settle here and if at all you need anything, please ask. Jassi will get you something to eat and some tea. Welcome, Mr. Nakul.'

A home is not a home until a woman walks in. A man without a woman is a man without a home. This new place began to feel like home and pretty soon a tall, salwar lady with a purple dupatta, Jassi, joined the new guests offering them halwa and tea. The luggage was helped in by men of the truck. Sukhwinder himself monitored the luggage being brought in. The house of the sardar bore a festive look. Chairs were drawn in from corners of sardar's house and all the adults settled in for some chit-chat. The young children were somewhat ignored as they ran around their house trying to find places to hide. Sardar's sons were not at home but were expected soon.

'Sir, I have been to many places as a young cadet, even before I got married. But I must say that there is something about the Punjab that fills me with the spirit of youth, for I think it is the land of the bravest. This is the second time I have been here but never in a village like this. The people are so warm and industrious, it reflects in their thumb of green. No matter what happens, this place will be home for travellers like us. I have already found my family, thank you, sir, you are very kind.'

'Mr. Nakul, what can I say about this land and our country. We all have learnt to live together as one, what happens around us will not come in our way of friendship. I am most humbled by your feelings for the Punjab. I just want to be a good neighbour, and treat you like my own brother. If I carry on, I may not be able to hold back my tears, for what I feel about the armed forces and its valiant men and women. You are most welcome here.'

No one looked at the sky above and pretty soon it was dark. The two families were at their respective homes, resting and ready to sleep after a very long day. The kids were already asleep in their room that was untidy, dusty, a total wreck with just the bed in order. Nakul and Radha had been awake in a separate room having a last cup of tea. Their room too required a lot of work and they just managed to get a bed with a mattress. They were not aware of what the new day would bring. Nakul knew his way to his office and Radha had already fixed a maid. The children were the worst hit. Their school, like it had been before always, was twenty kilometres away from home. They were allowed a day of rest before joining school.

Joginder, the younger son was all of sixteen. Parminder was in college and chose to stay on the hostel. Jogi, as he was fondly called by his mother, loved to stay at home and watch Chitrahar (show of Hindi songs), on Wednesdays. The family had managed to purchase a colour television, quite a revelation in the neighbourhood. Soon Jogi's eyes fell on Suresh, the hooter of his family but way younger than him. Naresh was uptight and did not open up to strangers very easily. Jogi, his lovely long hair, tied into a boy-turban, did not break into Punjabi, knowing that the new guests came from a different land. Soon the two were found running together around the courtyard, into Jogi's house and his small garden. Jogi and his brother were very fond of hockey. There were quite a few hockey sticks dangling on the walls of Jogi's drawing room. Sometime Jogi invited Suresh for a dual in his garden. Suresh, carrying the cricket bug like all of the children in India do, found it hard to grip the hockey stick. The hockey ball was unusually large, white and very hard. Suresh first followed Jogi as he dribbled the ball changing the sides of the hockey stick at will. When it was his turn to guide the ball, he just smacked it hard, sometimes hurting his opponents' legs. Jogi did not mind it as he made his way, with one leg, into his house. Jogi began to appreciate Suresh and talk to him on sensitive topics. The two spent a lot of time together, exchanging notes of their respective schools. Jogi was his mother's boy, totally obedient, taking to the broom each day to clear the garden of dry leaves and other trash. There was a discipline that Jogi and his brother stuck to, never opening their mouth when their parents lost their cool and harped on the things that were missing and ought to be addressed by the boys. Sometimes Jogi even did the dishes, cleaned the house and sat down with his mother to read the Holy text. Suresh watched all this with his eyes and learnt a lot from Jogi. His behaviour towards his parents was not up to the mark, he felt, and that he must get rid of his stupidity and obstinacy as he grew older. Jogi once produced his biology practical notebook to Suresh. There were some beautiful sketches of some wild animals lie the frog, turtle, bear that stunned Suresh's eyes. They were so beautifully drawn that Suresh could never forget them for years. What an artist Jogi was, and the purity of his soul, like the divine. Jogi let his hair down on Sundays as he played a game of badminton with Suresh and the boys in the courtyard.

The black day arrived. The radio broke the news and the T.V. played solemn tunes all day. There was a strange silence all over the village. The boys were into their games not knowing what it meant. Jogi was serious and knew more than others. It did not dent the camaraderie between the two families separated by a wire mesh door. They sat together in silence and sometimes spoke of the incident. Life was still defined by new mornings and darker evenings. Jogi and Suresh stood at the terrace one evening, when

Jogi broke the sad news. He and his family were moving to Chandigarh. Suresh somehow knew that he would never see Jogi again. Both friends stood in silence, trying to avoid each other's eyes. Jogi returned home that evening, never to be seen again. Nakul was ecstatic one cold morning, he had found a place at the Adampur Air Force station. The family was to move very soon.

Suresh never forgot the village all his life, and the cold 'Mattha' (drink of milk and curd churned) in the mornings. Many years later when he grew up to be a young man and came to understand all about 1984, he was sad. Jalandhar even then never lost the warmth of its people and the bravery with which each sardar faced life. It was the becoming of a great nation and its people, that knew the road to a peaceful existence, in spite of the difference in its brethren. Jogi, a beautiful lad from the Punjab, carried the 'Sanskar' that this entire nation is proud of.

# EARLY MELODY

LOVE

The third transfer of Sq. Ldr. Narendra Kumar to Bamrauli Air Force Station, Allahabad. The year was 1979 and his second son was all of five. A crisp khaki unform with the requisite batches of honour and a khaki cap with the eagle, black shoes, was enough to elicit a stern salute of the passing soldier of lower rank. Narendra seemed to ignore such honour, becoming of a senior officer. The Air Force Station covered acres of land as a prohibited area. No civilian could enter it without prior permission. Narendra was always on his feet, and presented more as an angry young man. His short temper was related partly to his blood and partly to the latent failures of a young man approaching forty. Marriage was the obvious hindrance and added to that the responsibility of two little boys. Narendra could not understand why every man has to follow a set path and feel incomplete in some ways. A routine path always led to more sorrow and a kind of enslavement to life. Sometimes he just wanted to run away from his wife and children. The burden was too big with no possibility of self-growth and higher accomplishment. He was trapped in a life that just happened to be, where, he thought, he had very little say. But married life did bring small pleasures and moments of happiness and composure. Children did bring laughter once in a while through their innocence and a devoted wife with her care made a beautiful home.

Roli, the younger lad, had taken to the waters like a cake walk. The elder son, Roni was rather quiet and played the more sensible kind. Narendra, a hard task master, did not spare the boys. However, there was a difference in how each boy received his wrath. Narendra was an honest man from birth. He could not tolerate fraud and lack of sincerity at work. There were discrepancies even in the working of the Armed Forces and people tried to take undue advantage of their rank and position. Narendra's honesty was clearly reflected in the paperwork he dealt with in the Logistics Department. Any deliberate attempt at hiding figures and quoting an incorrect data produced burning anger in Narendra and a possibility of essential hypertension. He then came home fuming and poured his anger on his family members. His wife Maya often said that it was like making a mountain out of a mole hill. Yet incessant parties at the Air Force Mess brought out a different side of Narendra. The couple attended many night parties where the children were not allowed. Narendra was a charming man, a most graceful man that the officers had ever seen. The ladies were awe struck, for when Narendra spoke with a glass of wine in his hand, a throng of people surrounded him and listened to the most wonderful tales that he narrated with pin drop silence. His bag of stories never went dry and he was especially called in such parties, especially by his seniors, to put life into the evenings and bring a smile on faces, grim with work. For when Narendra smiled the glasses went up for a toast for happiness and health to officers and their families. The charisma, delight, grace and beauty that Narendra possessed was never forgotten by officers and helped them carry on in an uncertain life that could end anytime the nation called on them for duty. How can a man shine like a jewel carrying a depth of life experience that no one could gauge. A man that often smiled at parties but burnt in fire for the rest of the time. For nothing but pain can make a man and bring out the true human embedded within. Narendra was always silent about his past and even Maya knew a fraction of his sufferings that he faced growing up. It is God's grace that keeps people alive in spite of the challenges and pain that each one goes through.

Roli was almost six when he first got admission in St. Xavier's College, an all-boys school along with his Roni. Each day began with the boys running haywire at the sound of Maya's voice. They were up at the first call, knowing that Narendra could take matters in his own hands very soon. Narendra would yell like a general cussing at his young troops in the field and could use the dreaded cane if required. When Narendra was done with his morning tea and a quick glance at the newspaper, he entered the boy's room. The boys stood in a line in full school uniform their ties in hand for Narendra to put a swift knot on them. Narendra used this opportune time to address the boys,

"Look here you rats, please walk by the side of the road holding hands, Roni please take care of that. Listen to what the teacher says at school, I don't want any complaints. For if you don't obey orders then you will be squished like a rat under the tyres of a huge truck. Please remember, I am watching you all the time, be good, do not ever cheat. Off you go, the tie is done."

Roni was of the serious kind. He detested his father's instructions and behaviour somewhere deep inside. He felt that his father was rude and did not care for his children.

'A cane is not the answer to all life questions, after all we are humans and not his rats meant for experiments'.

Roni never put a foot wrong deliberately and so Narendra hardly ever caused him much harm. He just left the lad without any scar or admonition.

Roli was totally opposite of Roni and that's why perhaps Narendra loved him a lot more than Roni. Roni was the mother's lad, ideal in all possible ways. Narendra would put his heavy head and body on little Roli's stomach, to watch Roli squirm and push Narendra out of his body. Narendra often played the harmonica before Roli and Roli would smile sweet. Roli was never upset with Papa's ways. He just wanted to play around with him. So, as soon as he heard Papa's footsteps approaching the door he would spill some water near the dining table, or break a piece of costly cutlery, or spill some food outside his eating plate. Papa boiled over with anger when he saw the damage. Then a loud noise of a tight slap across Roli's face and Roli cried aloud feeling the darkness around his eyes. Papa would retire to his room and Maya would hold the little boy and wipe his tears. Roli felt a sudden warmth in his heart each time Papa poured his wrath on the boy. Somewhere in his heart he was convinced that Papa loved him a lot and the act was just a drama. He was thus not scared of facing Narendra, the nemesis to Roni. Papa would often offer bananas after hitting his boy too hard,

'O! baby, I am sorry, did I hit you too hard. Papa is a bad man, just forgive him, my poor baby, I'll never hit you again, I promise'.

But the cane never stopped, the slaps came even harder as work pressure grew and sometimes even Roli was convinced that Papa was a devil and did not love him at all.

The family never forgot that night. The weather was cool outside as December set in. Narendra introduced a new member in the family. There was a medal for Narendra's exceptional service during war and a huge stylish green bottle of French perfume with it. Narendra and Maya were to go to a party in the evening thrown by Narendra's juniors in his honour. Narendra was very excited that day and couldn't take his eyes off his medal, and the huge perfume bottle which he thought shouldn't be opened too soon. Maya was busy all day sorting her sarees for the evening party. The clock struck seven and the huge wait was over. Narendra and Maya left the house for the party on Narendra's scooter. Roli was amused by the perfume bottle and never left its sight. The children had been warned not to enter Papa-Mummy's room at all. Just then there was a huge crashing sound. The huge perfume bottle had slipped from the hands of Roli, while he tried to feel it, and scattered to a million pieces on the floor. The door bell then rang, and the boys were sweating in fear. Roli ran to the door and opened it. Papa was at the door,

'Is everything alright? Don't worry, we'll be back very soon, please take care Roni.'

Papa did not enter the house as he turned around for the scooter in a helmet. Roli closed the door and the boys ran to Papa's room that had scattered green glass on the floor. The perfume smell was very strong and it made the boys dizzy. Roni quickly took some soap from the bath room and gave Roli instructions,

'Roli let's scrub the floor with soap, I'm sure the smell will go away and I need the broom to clear the scattered glass.' The cleaning process lasted for hours and the boys finally managed to bring the room to the way it was earlier. The strong fragrance of the French perfume did not leave the room completely. The boys were anxious and did not want Papa and Mummy to get home too soon. They stood at the window silently watching for the appearance of Papa and Mummy. At half past twelve, after midnight, the boys heard the noise of a scooter engine, approaching the window. It was Papa and Mummy. The boys rubbed their eyes and sweat covered their face out of fear. Roni opened the door as Narendra with sleepy eyes walked in followed by Maya. Narendra found out what had happened immediately,

'Where are you rascals, where is the bottle of French perfume, I cannot see it, what happened?'

Boys were looking down with shame and great fear.

'I said, what happened to the bottle, answer me, or I shall whip you today with my belt.'

Roli, head down, murmured,

'It slipped out of my hands'.

'Do you know why that bottle was given to me. I'm sure you don't. I am not going to spare you today, dirty rat'.

Then came the onslaught of slaps and kicks and the final whip across Roli's tender chest.

'Don't you dare enter my room again. No food for this guy for the entire day tomorrow. You think I fool around, going to office and working hard. Do you even know what goes on in my life or your mother's life. Do you know how hard we work each day for you guys. Baseless rogues you are, heartless children, good for nothing. Remember these words when I tell you, none of you will ever succeed in life, no matter what you do, please go to hell'.

Roli was crying at the top of his voice. He was badly hurt in body and soul. Maya held the boy and took him to his room. The lights of the house were on for almost the entire night. No family member ever slept that night. Roni was quiet and felt sorry for his brother.

This incident shook Roli completely. He never saw any wrong in his father, only in himself. How could he destroy someone's dreams, someone's honest work. Roli never left his room after this incident. After school he stayed in his room the rest of the day. He never entered Papa's room or even glance at it when he was called for food. He never deliberately did anything to bring Papa's wrath. He held a serious and pensive face all day long. In school he was very quiet and skipped games during recess. Narendra did not like what he saw and the silence in the house was unbearable. Narendra called Roli to his room one evening,

'Roli, come, good Lord there is so much of sweat on your face. Here, let me wipe it off. Look Roli, please forgive me for what I said. I don't mean a word, son, it just came out. Try to understand it's sometimes hard to be an adult and face the world. You are only aware of this battle that I fight each day at office. You are probably unaware of the infinite battles in my mind at the moment. Look besides you guys, I have to take care of a lot of other people in my family, for I am the eldest son. And your mother, I have not been good to her and she has a huge list of complaints. People play at lot of games my son, which you are unaware of. I hope you could walk in my shoes, son. I don't want to burden you with anything, you are just a baby. Have fun, my dear, enjoy your life. Growing up is the rule, you will enter that phase one day. Life is not roses, son. Please be yourself, do not mind your old man and his words. Be happy, please go and let's have the mayhem again'.

Roli never wanted to be a grown up, he never had any plans for the future. He knew one thing, Papa and Mummy loved him and he loved them too.

The games carried on for four more years until Narendra was given a transfer. Roli loosened himself again. His hands never stayed still and the list of broken things piled up. Papa's harsh words, slaps, and whips never ceased. He cursed the boys even more. And Roli just loved to be with Papa and knew exactly how to call for his company. Roli sometimes read Papa's face and how he pretended to spill his wrath on the boys, smiling away as he turned around.

'I got you this time', Roli knew it all.

Roni was not amused. He did not like so much chaos in the house and had known long ago that his father was abusive. Being quiet was the way out so that no one could blame him for anything.

Love grew each day. Roli's greatest heroes were Narendra and Maya. Roli spent hours looking at old pictures of the couple's marriage and their fun ride during honeymoon. Papa would carry Roli on his shoulders, like a crown.

Love is the greatest emotion and will be forever. It is learnt in our first ever school called Home of Mummy and Papa. True love is hard to find but can be possible if we learn to love our parents. Let's bend and be willing to learn. Our parents, the greatest heroes, are teaching us how to live. They are here for us, to protect us, guide us and take us to the most unimaginable place one can ever think of.

# A TALE OF TWO TOWERS

CONFUSION OF TOWERS

Great men produce weak sons. Nirmal, a man with the magic glow, had seen dismal days that hung on for too long. The man with a genius brain, could reach out for solutions as remote as the Himalayan peak. He was 'the' man to talk to. Philosophy, literature, psychology melted like the clear water of the Gangotri. How can a man with a fetish for romantic novels and Dona Summer know such things as deep as the abyss. Such clarity and preciseness of thought was certainly not his dream, they just happened. When Nirmal's father called him on one quiet night to his study, Nirmal, raw and never a rebel in the making, was a little puzzled.

'Nirmal, my son, I hope the weather is treating you right. This is going to be brief; I don't know anything about circles, I have a photograph. This is a girl that lives in a small town far from here. I happened to meet his father while I was at work. He too works for a different district as an ADM, same as my position. It's a good family and your mother and me want to meet the family.'

'Babuji, I have recently joined the military and I think we should wait for some time. Is that possible?'

Nirmal stopped and presented a blank face,

'Do I look like the marriage type, Babuji, I am destined for greener pastures' Nirmal uttered the words to himself.

'Please don't ask questions, we have made up our minds, and we are not turning back' Babuji was very clear.

Twelve years into marriage and Nirmal was burdened by two sons, one of ten and the other of eight. Nirmal knew the road to excellence, the road to calm, the road to clarity of thought and expression, the road to fulfilment and that it all came at a hefty price. His children were bound to crack under the load if at all they tried to be themselves in completeness. He knew that the development process is very painful and the blows of the hammer, chisel was not for the weak hearted. It takes just one man to make a dive into the sea of gruesome currents and tides, enough to make him insane. Hence, he just wiggled his cup of tea calmly to mix the sugar settled at the bottom to the remaining tea. He combed his hair with a pocket comb that he always carried, staring at himself closely in the mirror. He pulled his trousers up and tucked his shirt in nicely before walking on where life would take him. He had given up a long time ago, when his father was ready with the photograph, too keen for the 'bahu'(daughter-in-law) and dreaming of being a grandfather. It's hard to explain anything to kids of ten or eight for it takes a lifetime to get anywhere and the realization is even farther away. Nirmal often gazed into nothing, expressionless and silent while his children made noises and ran around the house like children do.

Nirmal headed to his in-law's house during summer breaks always in that small town where his marriage was solemnized. His father-in-law was a reputed man in that town and also adjoining districts. He was a good man, a man of great principles with the shine of olden days. His wife, Kalawati, was a strong lady and a great fighter that managed the affairs of the house and also a lot of matters that exclusively belonged to the male club. Her daughter, Komal, Nirmal's wife was not as strong as her mother, yet had a great sense of duty and a touch of the olden times when promises were made and fulfilled to the extent of laying down lives for the word. Mahesh Babu, as his father-in-law was known was not happy with his life. Two daughters, Komal and Kamla were just about par with Komal the better of the two. His heart was broken by his three sons, that remained aloof from him and his wife for reasons that were sometimes hard to understand. There was nothing to learn from their renowned and respected father, nothing to decipher from the tales of bravery of great men that their mother narrated with a shine in her eyes and a pleasing smile. They were on the wrong road; Mahesh Babu knew that from the beginning. He just sat with Kalawati in their room late into the night when the children were asleep and did not utter a word. Kalawati had known the truth way before her husband. She just blamed the new era that had dawned suddenly, and brought with it its own sick values. Mahesh Babu could hold the ship as long as he was alive and live with desperation and defeat but was not sure about what might happen afterwards. He could never understand why none of his children never even had the slightest curiosity to know what his parents were all about. He remembered how he gave up his life for his father and always obeyed his word. He was fast coming to the conclusion that the golden period of this land was over and the ones to come would be a complete waste. Real joy, he felt, comes after a hard day. If the hard day is given up for a life of merry making then no true son will be born out of the soil. Mahesh Babu's hair turned grey in thought while Kalawati made sure to dye her hair and linger as an optimist. Mahesh Babu shared the same sentiments as Nirmal when it came to the plight of their children. Nirmal, however, was not as disappointed as his father-in-law. He knew that life was not meant for everyone to conquer and every kid that came was bound to be lost into the greater fair emerging in the distance. He was quite calm when it came to such matters and would rather enjoy the strong tea that his wife prepared. He believed that sons are not sons anymore but they must have them for continuity. Komal was a big fan of her father, a very rare sight for Mahesh Babu. She was hesitant to enter his room as a child and now her husband made it easier to walk in with greater ease. She offered tea to her father and sat with him with bated breath to hear some words of wisdom and perhaps some encouragement. A slightest mistake in carrying the word of her father and she cursed herself for the rest of her life. She liked the culture of cleanliness that her father inculcated in his children. He would himself take the broom and sweep the floor when the children refused to do the same. At such times Komal snatched the broom from her father and made sure she cleaned the room to her father's expectations. Mahesh Babu always told his children to clean their rooms at the end of the day before going to sleep. That way they all would wake up to a clean room giving them good thoughts. Mahesh Babu's bed had clean white sheets on them, his kurta was crisp, white and clean and so was his dhoti. Kalawati was not very keen to stay neat and clean but she made sure that their bedroom looked just the way her husband wanted.

It was a busy morning in the small town where Mahesh Babu lived. Nirmal as usual had come with his boys and wife to spend the summer holidays. Nirmal was not very enthusiastic to visit his in-laws but had to give in to Komal's wishes. That day Mahesh Babu had left for office. Nirmal happened to be at the neighbour's house for chit-chat. Naresh and Nakul, the two sons of Nirmal were in their Nana's(grandfather) room. Kalawati never missed a smile when she saw the boys. Komal joined the boys with Kalawati.

'What do you want to do, children. Have some snacks and tea. You must be bored here with no one to talk to or play with. Why don't you go out and look around, see what you can find here. I know this town is not as good as your city, but you'll like it, I bet.' Kalawati smiled at the boys and the boys looked at each other.

'Naresh, Nakul, Nani is right. Go and see, there is a temple across the road. And please hold each other's hand when crossing the road. Naresh, please help Nakul.' Komal pushed the boys for a spin.

There was a narrow lane outside the house that ended with the main road. Naresh and Nakul were not sure if they really wanted to go out, instead of those huge yellow ladoos hiding in the big glass jar in granny's kitchen. Naresh, the wiser of the two pushed Nakul, like it was a question of their self-respect, to prove that they were capable explorers. Nakul just wanted to look at her Nani all day, in her sweet smile and tender words, those big ladoos of despair, and the glorious food that even Komal could not prepare. The boys reached the end of the narrow lane to enter the main road. Naresh took to the right and Nakul followed not far behind. The busy street had dhoti clad men on bicycles with mouth of paan (betel leaf) and different ways of injecting tobacco into that preparation. Walkers, some young, some old, some with dhotis, walking like on a mission. There were very few cars and whenever one happened to pass by, the streets were blocked and the people in the cars were stared at and cursed silently. The age-old rickshaw saw stout woman and little children being pulled by wiry black men, again with dhotis, with not enough strength to pull it forward. And there were the first timers like Naresh and Nakul who did not know where they were headed. The passing time took them to a tower which they were familiar with. It stood at the crossroads and had a thinking Gandhi sitting at the centre. The boys just walked and walked with Nakul's mouth watering at the sight of hot samosas and jalebis. He ran to Naresh and requested him to spare some change. Naresh too could not stop himself and the two sat in a small eating place that had benches to sit on and a table to serve food. The boys were served hot jalebis and samosas as they looked around trying to make some sense of the mayhem around them. Naresh promptly pulled out some cash and paid for the delicious snack. The boys were in no mood to go any further, suspecting nothing better in the road ahead. Naresh quietly asked Nakul,

'Let's go home. Look, I can see the tower right in front of me. It means that we have to go straight for some distance and turn left into the narrow lane. That lane, as we all know, will reach us home. Let's go, I can't bear this nonsense around me.'

The boys heavy with untimely snack in their stomach pushed their steps forward with force. They walked for some distance with their eyes turned to the left for the narrow lane. The elusive narrow lane never arrived and the boys were sweating with anxiety.

'Nakul, what happened to the narrow lane? Where are we, do you have any idea. Maybe, we should go back to the tower and try walking this way again.'

The boys turned back and ran to the tower in quick steps, the taste of heavy snack long forgotten. They started from the tower again and walked slowly with eyes to the left,

'Walk slow Nakul, I'm sure we missed it last time.'

This time too there was no left lane and Nakul was almost in tears,

'What will we do now, will we ever get back home. Getting out was a bad idea, I mean we do not belong to this place, Da.'

Both kids were tired with one with his hands on his knees and the other totally on the ground, not caring about the dust smeared on the shorts.

'We are lost Nakul, I am sorry I pushed you, I just cannot figure this out.'

The boys did not move for hours until evening. Nakul's eyes were dry after crying softly and Naresh had no words of commiseration. The boys started walking straight with no hope of ever getting home. They maintained some distance between each other and were like destitute kids who could not ask for help. Twenty steps later, Naresh saw something unbelievable,

'Nakul this is another tower. Look it has Gandhi sitting at its centre. This is the tower we were looking for. How stupid can we be, there are two towers, Nakul. The other one did not have a Gandhi at its centre.'

The boys raced forward beyond the tower with the Gandhi at its centre. The narrow lane to the left suddenly appeared and the boys shouted aloud in excitement. They reached home in a jiffy and tried to forget all that had happened.

Kalawati and Komal stood outside the main gate, worried for the kids. They were more than happy to receive them.

'What happened kids, what took you so long. Have you travelled the entire town on foot?' Kalawati was quick to ask them.

'Nani, we went to the tower at the crossroads that has a Gandhi at its centre and by accident overshot to another tower that looked similar. We could not figure out that there were two towers not too far from each other. We got confused and hence could not get home in time.'

Kalawati laughed aloud,

'Oh! My little babies, there are indeed two towers here. But children it should not have taken so much time to figure out that there were two, for both of them are very close to each other. Your children are something, Komal, such innocence is hard to find these days.'

Mahesh Babu, Nirmal heard about the incident and it brought a smile to their faces.

Hope never died with Nirmal and Komal when it came to their children. Mahesh Babu and Kalawati did see something in the boys.

In a crafty world where people make plans just to harm others and boys become men in no time, it was good to see a whiff of innocence somewhere. However, the world is a very cruel place and no one is spared, unless one finds an easy way through life by deception, lies and constant crimes. The innocent are God's own children and have to pay a heavy price for existence. Freedom is the final word and no one has ever dared to reach the final door, darkness is just a way of life.

# GUITAR LESSONS

A PERFECT MELODY

A man without music cannot hear silence. Mahesh loved songs and music. His interest in anything English led him to those singers of the west that lived in an era of rebellion. That line of thought had seeped into India with great force and cases of self-exploration against established norms was quite common. Yet Mahesh was not one of them. He obeyed his father and soon became the father of two meaningless children. One could still hear the soothing and provocative voice of Dona Summer with bits of Cliff Richard, Simon & Garfunkel and the beautiful Scott McKenzie through his window. In those times of the beginning of the eighties a tape recorder by Nelco was a rare and prized possession. A dip of the cassette into the slot with a nostalgic sound of closing the dome and a push of the majestic play button made music much like making love. Years may come and go, everything may change to the miniscule, new people may come in, but a tape recorder is a romance that people of that era can never forget. The boys usually hung on to Cliff Richard and his 'Bachelor Boy' but Mahesh only connected with Donna Summer. She was a mystery to the stupid boys and Mahesh kept his love, hidden far away in the corners of his almirah. The boys just could not understand the words of English numbers and the title of the song perhaps was the only thing that sounded familiar in the song. English songs were thrust on the boys at a very early age and they ruined the tape recorder by pushing the rewind button too often. Mahesh reached a stage in his life when he was far away from music. The work demanded endless hours in the office where the ceiling fan was the only music to the ear. In spite of the drought his love for music never died and he could picture his college days when as a young man he would dance alone in his room to who else but Donna. Marriage and the boys had taken the romance from his life and the fetters of responsibility had stolen his dancing shoes. Mahesh wanted his children to experience the magic of music. He was happy to see broken cases of cassettes and a tape recorder that did not produce any music anymore. He believed that the sounds heard in childhood could never be forgotten and it would push them towards learning the English language. What else can a man do but pass on his love to his children. Songs are the hardest to decipher, he believed, for the words are casual with a tinge of slang and are sung like a man intoxicated with wine. Indians, he knew, found it very hard to read the lips of English singers and sometimes the ignorance lasted for an entire lifetime. He felt it's not right to catch the lyrics in a book, the real beauty of the song is in listening carefully until the words make complete sense, especially those hidden by the lip. Mahesh hoped that one day music would find a special place in the lives of the boys, it would be a complete shame if it eluded their ears completely. Time and again Mahesh introduced some new singers as the years passed by and a sixties singer appeared to have started his career in the eighties in India. The Beatles, Dorris Day were introduced much later and the boys sat in wonder with crisp sounds of drums, guitar, et al into their young ears.

Mahesh wanted the boys to play some musical instrument. The school stuff was not enough and the boys were anyway below average in studies. Extra-curricular activities were beyond them and they would rather die as dumb than utter words to impress some crowd. A teacher far away gave Hawaiian guitar lessons. Mahesh thought this as a good way to introduce a musical instrument into the lives of the boys. Mahesh sometimes during those long Sundays picked up the harmonica, lying on the bed with the children, and played such delightful tunes, whamming his hands in quick succession. The boys were impressed by Mahesh's talent that was always hidden under his grim face.

One evening on a Saturday, Mahesh with his two sons on a scooter and a guitar inside a hard case on one of the boy's laps drove all the way to the teacher's residence. It was about five kilometres away. A Bengali man in kurta and pyjama with a red mouth of paan and a deep black moustache greeted them at the door. He intermittently poked some naswaar (powdered tobacco) into his nose and his smile could not hide his red wrecked teeth.

'Come Babu, I was waiting for you. Mr. Mahesh the boys are safe in my hands. I'll make them expert guitarists. Please have patience and don't show up in less than two hours from now to take them home. You can leave now; these boys look good.'

The boys were expecting a guitar hanging on a strap around their shoulders in a standing position as they gently plucked the strings with fingers of the right hand, while the left hand danced on the frets. They thought that that was the only kind of guitar present in the world of music. Yet the teacher asked them to sit comfortably on the diwan and placed the guitar on their laps. He took out a steel bar and placed it between their middle finger and the index finger of the left hand with the supporting thumb at the bottom. In the right hand a series of steel rings that were heavy and each finger had one on it. The boys were disillusioned and from the very beginning they wanted to run away. They did not accept the nice smile on the teacher's face with his intermittent naswaar making him perky and hopeful from lost causes.

The initial lessons were too boring for the boys and they did not know why the teacher was making them do such silly things with the guitar strings. For example,

'Go 1-2-3-4-5-6, 1-6, 2-5, 3-4, 1-2-3, 3-2-1...' the teacher went on continuously looking at the plucking of the strings like the boys were creating something unusual. The bare hands plucked the strings for forty-five minutes,

'Boys, please trim your nails, you don't need long dirty nails, look what do we have here, two cups of hot tea and some sweet biscuits to go with it. Let's take a break.'

The boys were relieved and came to the conclusion that learning an instrument was not as hard as the teacher thought it was. Plucking the strings for hours was pointless and the boys wanted to jump in to the exciting part of playing tunes of popular songs from the 'weeping' guitar. They were once again asked to do what they had been doing so far, waiting for the scooter of Papa.

'O! Mr. Mahesh, your sons are a genius, they learnt the initial lessons so quickly, I think they will master the instrument in no time. Goodbye, see you again.'

Home was a big relief for the boys and the guitar lay in its box till the next class.

Many classes followed and the teacher was adamant at making the boys pluck the strings for hours. The boys could not complain against the teacher to anyone, too scared of Mahesh and their mother could hold no secrets. Every time the class ended, the teacher sang in praise of the boys,

'Wonderful boys, they are picking up the lessons at great speed and will become masters soon.'

Three weeks passed and the boys were still plucking strings, but this time they had a tinge of a rebel in their eyes and when they looked at the teacher, he pushed his naswaar deeper that he usually did and started in a light tone,

'Boys, I have a surprise for you, today you will pick up that steel bar and push steel rings on your middle and index fingers, and I shall teach you Sargam.'

'Go Sa-Re-Ga-Ma-Pa-Dha-Ni-Sa. Sa-Ni-Dha-Pa-Ma-Ga-Re-Sa. Once again, Sa-Re-Ga...'

The boys were delighted and the sound of the Hawaiian guitar was like the sadness of the soul.

'Mr. Mahesh your boys are a genius, they are too good.'

Five and a half months and all that the boys did was play Sargam for two hours. The teacher never taught them any further. It took the eyes of fire of the famished boys for the teacher to teach them a song tune, finally. But it was too late, this was their penultimate class. And the teacher went,

'My God, Mr. Mahesh your boys are too good. What beautiful hands. I have never seen such geniuses in my life.'

And the song was a popular number in Indian film music,

'Bekarar karke hume Un Na Jaiye...'. (Please don't leave me in such desperation, come back, my beloved).

The tune was picked up with a additional class that was forcefully arranged by the teacher on the request of the boys.

'Sir, your boys have overwhelmed me, they are so good. Ask them to practice the song and remember me when they play it. Goodbye, Mr. Mahesh, it was a pleasure.'

All the boys learnt after six months of hard work, going to and fro with that heavy guitar on the lap, was a paltry one song. Were they supposed to play just one song for the rest of their lives?

It so happened that they abandoned the guitar after some time except that tune that remained fresh somewhere in their minds.

And about that Bengali teacher that was so enthusiastic about the boys- Mahesh found out that there was a huge tender that Air Force had invited for offer a year ago. That Bengali teacher wanted his organization to get the tender bid and when the time arrived, Mahesh spoke highly about the teacher while acting as the officer of allotment of the tender. And thus, the sweet cheat Bengali teacher got the tender to his name.

Mahesh knew in his heart that the boys were good for nothing. It would be a miracle if one of the boys could develop some taste for good music in the future, playing an instrument was not in their blood.

# LADIES AT BAMRAULI

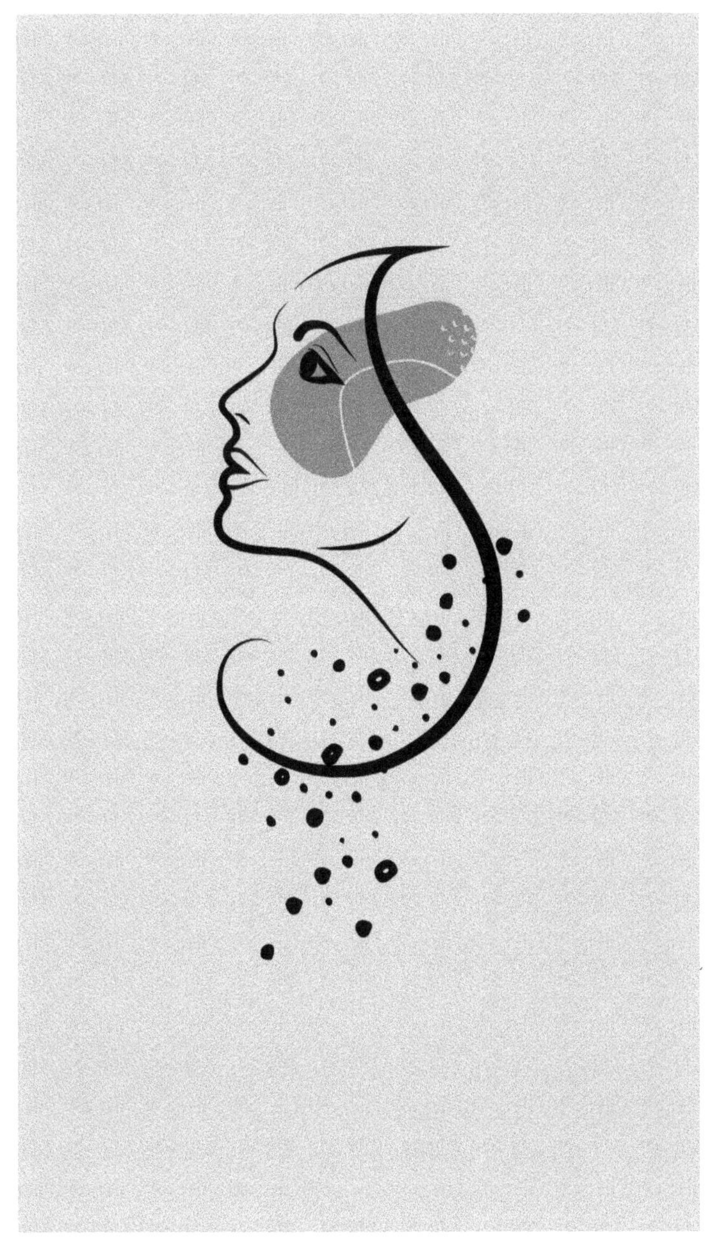

THE LADIES

The Air Force Bamrauli ladies in the early eighties were devoted wives. That was not a balloon era like this one when women want to be men. Their home was a place called paradise. Each lady lent a distinct fragrance to their home that was quite evident when someone came along for an evening to that home. There were no raging wars, no poverty to speak of, although each one survived on a tight budget. There was no feeling of hostility anywhere and the women never felt any discontentment or being denied of their fundamental rights. They were real craftswomen at work – while someone was an expert at cooking new dishes, someone created rare patterns on cloth, or some did paintings for the wall, or some with creative jute work, etc. No one could define the limits for the ladies and they closely coordinated with each other to share and work on a daunting masterpiece.

Mrs. Chaddha was clever and did not leave any opportunity to cheat or take a slight advantage off other women. Mrs. Bannerji was tall, slim and very fair. She wore track suits in the morning and ran around the Air Force campus with her long black hair left free to bounce in the air. She was a woman with a perpetual smile and it was no surprise that many men had a secret crush on her. She applied cream, turmeric paste and a host of other natural solutions on her face to keep it shining. A random visit to her house would invariably scare the person to the point of running away for she received the guest with her face covered in some solution making her look like a witch. She was, however, a very nice lady and knew just how to impress people with her dignified way of talk. She was known to be very good at heart and the ladies just loved her.

Mrs. Shastri lived next to Mrs. Bannerji and was a pure artist. She was a great learner and was known throughout the Air Force station to be very humble and to possess great optimism. Mrs. Mehta was a very sweet woman. She was not so tall, wore glasses, was slim, had a little daughter names Mili and proved to be a great wife and mother. Mrs. Shastri and Mrs. Mehta were great friends and just could not stay apart for too long, although they lived at some distance from each other. Mrs. Dhillon was a typical Punjabi lady. She was a high-spirited woman but a little business oriented like Punjabis are. Mrs. Mukherji was perhaps the most talented woman in the entire Air Force Station. A very strong woman who had mastered many skills like cooking, knitting, painting and making charcoal images on frames. She was the leader of the ladies and spoke first when the ladies had a meeting or when some message was required to be passed to a higher authority. Mrs. Chaddha did not know her initially but stuck to her like parasite when Mrs. Shastri once introduced her to Mrs. Mukherji. She purposely came closer to Mrs. Mukherji in order to take advantage of the popularity that Mrs. Mukherji had. Mrs. Mukherji was a friend of Mrs. Shastri. She liked her honesty and a simple and direct approach to life. Mrs. Shastri learnt a lot of things from her and exchanged words in silence about matters that were important and carried weight in their lives. Mrs. Shastri had influenced Mrs. Mukherji in a positive way and Mrs. Mukherji always wanted to be with her whenever possible. There were ladies that were hardly ever noticed like Mrs. Iyer, Mrs. Sunderajan, Mrs. Nandan. They did not attend meetings or went to anybody's for the evening, but liked to be in their house all the time.

Mrs. Chadda was known to be wealthy. Women hardly ever went to her house. She had a lot of artefacts and pieces of decoration that seemed to be very expensive. Her drawing room had vases of ceramic with a rich embroidered surface, fancy photo frames that were state of the art, carpets that seemed to be woven in expensive fabric, expensive toys for the children including a huge set of toy trains that ran on long tracks and had stations and signals for up and down of the trains, cutlery imported from Europe, etc. She also had works of art like a wall hanging out of jute, fancy bead work in a partition like a curtain, charcoal drawings on frames that was the make of Air Force ladies themselves, the chief of the artwork was Mrs. Mukherji. Mrs. Chadda was the first lady to fix a price for the artwork of the Air Force ladies that did not think of converting it into a bigger business. The truth about Mrs. Chadda was that her wealth had been acquired by cheating and deception, a little by her own husband at work and a little inherited from her family. Any casual visitor was fooled by the expansive talk of the couple, exaggerating things beyond their ken and glorifying their lies. Mrs. Mukerji and Mrs. Shastri knew their game from the very beginning and knew how miserable their lives were in the absence of guests to their drawing room. They knew the tricks and the deception that ruled their lips and the wisdom they pretended to possess made them the poorest couple at Bamrauli. It is adversity that gives words to lips and Mrs. Chadda and family had never had one. Their children had the image of the richest kids around, good in sports, confident, rich in language and etiquettes, good in studies, and also good at deception of the subtle kind, a rare perfection. One cannot forget the most essential element, especially in this country of ours, to make someone uncommon and of a higher society lending an air of sophistication, the command over the English language. Centuries may pass by, ages may come and go, but we can never get over as slaves of anything English. The words itself transports us to the heavens with that infamous twang that sets us apart from the milieu. Mrs. Chadda only spoke in English and when she did break into Hindi sometimes, the words had a tinge of English in them.

Mrs. Dhillon invited the ladies and family to Lohri every year. A huge fire was lit in the passage of Mrs. Dhillon's house and every body cracked some sweet rabri (sweet with sesame seed coating). There was song and dance as Mrs. Chadda searched for something exotic in Mrs. Dhillon's house that she could undermine with her own belongings. Generally, the husbands, kids, ladies forgot all about themselves to enjoy the occasion and the soft evening air. The presence of guests and the noise was uplifting for all and such an occasion was eagerly awaited each year.

Mrs. Shastri's husband Kamal was very harsh on his two boys. He never stopped comparing them with the two sons of Mrs. Chadda. Mrs. Shastri acted as a balm on the boys after they had been caned for the slightest of mistakes by Kamal. She did not care about Mrs. Chadda's boys. She felt that children that are pampered by their parents too much, ones that are applauded for nothing, ones that are allowed to do anything that they like to, ended up doing nothing in life. After all the real life of each child begins when they step into adulthood, which is imminent and not too far. Mrs. Chadda encouraged their two sons to be men and never shy away from their first kiss.

"Sorry to say, Mr. Shastri but your children are too shy. Look at my kids, they have all the qualities of men, maturing faster than boys usually do."

Mrs. Shastri just stayed away from the phony world of Mrs. Chadda as much as she could. That is the reason she was thankful to stay next to Mrs. Bannerji that was many blocks away from Mrs. Chadda.

Mrs. Chadda wanted to break the calm and growing popularity of Mrs. Shastri. But she did not know how to go about it. There was a cricket match organized in the lawns of the Air Force Mess. Teams were made among the local boys and coincidently Mrs. Chadda's younger son, Chandan a fast bowler, was in one of the teams and Mrs. Shastri's son, Nakul was in the opposite team. The first over was to be bowled by Chandan and the batsman to face him was Nakul. Chandan did not like Mrs. Shastri's boys just like her mother. He walked up to run up mark, turned around and ran towards the wicket. Nakul blinked his eyes swiftly and tightened the grip on the bat. Chandan threw the ball with all his force. It bounced somewhere at the centre of the pitch, rose high, and hit the chest of Nakul. He cried out in pain and was soon pulled out by Kamal, who was watching the match from close quarters. He took Nakul home and had some soft words and asked him to withdraw from the match.

Mrs. Chadda heard about the incident and was overjoyed. She gave a rousing welcome to her son that had taken three wickets and scored tons of runs and rubbed his back in affection.

Once the ladies were fed up with Mrs. Chadda and especially to hear about Mrs. Shastri's son. An urgent meeting was called, attended by Mrs. Shastri, Mrs. Mukherji, Mrs. Bannerji, Mrs. Mehta,

Mrs. Dhillon and some others but not Mrs. Chadda. It was a late afternoon call when the ladies were totally free from familial duties. Mrs. Mukerji began,

"Ladies, I have called you today for a special meeting. We have found that Mrs. Chadda is trying to create a rift among friends by talking ill about some and extending loyalty to the ones that could benefit her. We must do something now; we cannot stand it anymore. So, I have come up with a plan and I am pretty sure that it will work. The Armed Forces annual day is upon us and besides the usual parade we throw a grand party attended by famous people of India and some foreign delegates too. For this year I shall give the responsibility of organizing the party entirely to Mrs. Chadda. I have heard her often say that she has some royal connections in England and that the French too in on her side. She has a lot of money and can undoubtedly make it even more lavish than what we have seen in the years gone by. Yes, Mrs. Shastri I can hear your giggle, but believe me Mrs. Chadda and her sweet family is one of the most elite and sought after, perhaps after the Queen of England. And just to remind you, Mrs. Chadda has often said to me privately that she can arrange the most fantastic show of glitter and glamour and that the ones arranged by us in the past was fit for those beggars on the streets of Patna. Ladies, please have some refreshments, arranged just for you and for the trouble you had breaking your normal daily routine."

Days passed in silence and it seemed that Mrs. Chadda was less of a threat to the harmony and peace of the Air Force station, Bamrauli. The ladies were busy with their lives and each one kept a quiet distance from each other.

On the 15$^{th}$ of December Mrs. Chadda received a man at her door with a circular in his hands. Mrs. Chadda promptly signed as received and the man was on his way out. There was no one at the house except her. The circular read,

"It is informed to Mrs. Chadda that she has been selected as the Chief Organizer of the Air Force Annual day party to be held on 25$^{th}$ of December in the lawns of the Air Force Mess and which also coincides with the Christmas Day celebrations. Congratulations! Air Force is very proud of the rich connections that Mrs. Chadda has and the promise she holds for organizing a feast beyond compare. If in case she does not fulfil her duties and fails to deliver what is expected of her then it will result in an immediate demotion and/or a transfer."

Mrs. Chadda dropped on a chair like a lightning had struck her. She had spread enough lies about her and the pomp and show were just a bigger lie. She never had any 'connections' at all. She never went to her village in the far east and had cut all ties with her near and dear ones because she thought they were too ancient for her. At the same time, it won't be right to spoil the image she had among the ladies and her children and husband helped her built this huge castle with no walls. Her husband spent all his time fooling around with the ladies with his tight and green glaze Rayban goggles. He hardly ever sat down and accomplished anything of worth and if not for his sweet talk in a polished accent, especially to his boss, he would have been kicked out a long time ago. He just burdened someone else's shoulders with his work promising them something exotic in return.

This time Mrs. Chadda was caught in her own web. She had never done such a thing before, all on her own, and she just enjoyed pulling someone down by calling them too rustic and uncouth. She loved to spark a fight among the ladies with her 'divide and rule'. When Mrs. Chadda gave this circular to her husband, he just threw his goggles away and cried in anger,

"What have you done, you stupid lady. Do you know what's going to happen. You don't know anything at all, they will transfer me to the interiors of Bihar or maybe to Ladakh. We are finished, all our royalty has been smashed to pieces and what do you think of our children. They will never learn anything new and develop in any way, very soon you may find them on Gutka and Khaini. O! God, best of luck with your preparation."

Mrs. Chadda did not give up until the last moment. There were about ten days left and she decided to keep quiet until the very end.

The ladies did not hear from her at all. On the fifth day Mrs. Chadda was called for an urgent meeting of the ladies. Mrs. Mukherji along with the others sat on chairs on a pleasant morning in the Air Force Mess.

"Mrs. Chadda, without any delay, we would like to know about your preparations for the annual day and the progress you have made so far. There are just five days left, we must hurry up, please!"

Mrs. Chadda got up from her chair, removed the bulky goggles from her eyes and stuck it over her head.

"Mrs. Mukherji and ladies, I am sorry to tell you that I have failed to make any progress in the matter. I will not lie, I don't have any connections anywhere except with the kind ladies of Air Force Station, Bamrauli. Please excuse me, I don't want to carry this burden any more. I resign from the post of the Chief Organizer of the Air Force Annual day party. And if you ladies don't mind, I must leave right away."

The ladies at the meeting had a sigh of relief.

Mr. Chadda was transferred to Trivandrum in the extreme south. It was far away from their homes. Mrs. Chadda lost all interest in life and the new place did not have the amenities she enjoyed at Bamrauli. There were hardly any families there and the Mess was barren with a bar not big enough to hold more than three bottles. There was no television, no pool or even a lawn. The children went to school that did not have many teachers or even a big enough building.

The ladies at Air Force station made a lot of progress in the coming years without the evil shadow of Mrs. Chadda. It was the time of their lives and each one promised to be in touch forever. There is an old adage of the Armed Forces that is true always - 'transfers are the rule'. One by one the ladies left Bamrauli to new places with their husbands and children.

A wise man once said, 'Don't give your heart to someone, for they will leave one day.'

# PLUNGE OF TRUTH

SATYAM SHIVAM SUNDARAM

Sq. Ldr. Neel Kumar completed fifteen years in the Indian Air Force. His proud moment, a commission by the then President Dr. S. Radhakrishnan. He began alone on this journey, flying low on a transport aircraft above Andaman and Nicobar Islands, catching corals from underneath the sea. His stay at Coimbatore was a never to forget experience. Soon he was joined by his wife Mala and two sons Kamal and Vimal. By that time, he had become a north bird, living at places like Jalandhar, New Delhi and finally Bamrauli Air Force station, Allahabad. As a sign of a well to do family and profession, his khaki shirt buttons were tight to the limit around his stomach and chest. Yet he was one of the most handsome men at Bamrauli. A casual walk during working hours in the campus elicited a salute of a lower rank officer or a sudden jerk to a straightened spine if on a bicycle. Neel had seen a lot of hardships in life, many hidden and weighing down on his eyes as he opened a new chapter in his life. Mala could never know the complete man and he often hummed his way out in grave discussions. If felt as if he had read the wave of life and nothing could upset him or raise an eyebrow. He worked his way through life with studied and still eyes, ready to ease the discomfort of the people around him. With life in his pocket, he was always ready to fall. A fall for the truth, righteousness, honesty, scary as it may sound, it was not meant for the faint hearted. Walking safe was not meant for travellers like Neel, he was the saviour of his seniors, battalion, ubiquitously sent on difficult missions, standing like a shield of armour to protect his people. Plenty were hidden in his own nest with knives, spears, hit from the back, on the sly, tribe. Such people, Neel knew, were gentle and kind, and killed sweetly by distortions of paper. It was a never-ending battle and Neel found solace when he was commended by high officers and was even given protection. Files piled up on his desk making him sometimes sleep in office at night. He made sure complete files and work done before time reached the desk of his seniors. Mala waited for him on such nights knowing where he would be. Those parties with ladies and their men were the most exciting for her. A night at the Air Force mess was like moments in paradise. The children were kept away for those occasions and the evening crafted in suits and tie for men, women in sarees, bar man dressed up in a turban, the soda out of shiny bottles, air with sweet perfumes and cigarette smoke, and laughter on every lip. These were the times when the men of the forces let go, all grievances, hatred and morning sirens calling for duty. Neel became the centre of attraction, with his jokes and laughter from his bag of tales and words decorated that went off the roof. Yet all agreed and laughter like a breeze spread all over. Hard drinks were a must which the ladies avoided, and it was no secret why the men in uniform could not live without it. Everyone waited for such parties and it came as a relief and a breather for duty bound men and women.

It was on the record that Neel never ever took even a pin home that belonged to the office. Such honesty was never seen or heard and sometimes it unsettled certain jealous men. Neel sometimes rued the fact that he had to work under a boss that was sometimes unfair. He was an obedient officer to his bosses but at times he got bad bosses. At one such occasion Group Captain (G.C.) Venkataswami was his immediate boss. G.C. Venkataswami had heard a lot about this young officer, Neel Kumar. His honesty and tales of bravery had reached G.C.'s ears. The way this officer was going up the rung of success, bothered him, making him green with envy. He knew that one day Sq. Ldr. Neel Kumar would become the Air Chief Marshal while he would be exactly where he is right now. He was eager to hone his malice and screw the young officer and even end his career. It was difficult to make a fool proof plan against Neel, for everyone trusted him a lot. But the final report of progress was totally in his hands and at the end of the year he could write as he wished. It so happened that G.C. Venkataswami and his wife came to stay in the same building as Neel and his family. G.C. and his wife lived on the ground floor while Neel occupied the first floor. G.C. had no children and there was a sense of grief in his heart shared equally by his wife. G.C. sat up many nights in the guise of official work while he planned the downfall of Neel, with a burning pipe for his company. His wife objected to the lights not being turned off at night for which the G.C, stayed at the office for some nights. He carefully checked the papers prepared by Neel, signed by him, and the blue stamp that embroidered all the papers. There was not even the slightest of discrepancies, and mistakes were too farfetched. He could not dig a hole into those papers and he was quite upset, holding those heavy nights on his shoulders. Neel handled the logistics and the supplies were never insufficient and the whole inventory was perfectly managed. There was no slack anywhere. The only option left for the G.C. was to create a fault by deception and ruin the young man's career. Hence, he forged some documents and interspersed it with the good ones so that it looked at a glance that all was well. The very next day he got up early and sat at his chair in crisp uniform, his pipe hissing a song of victory and called his subordinate. The dubious file was handed over and neatly placed at Neel's table before his arrival for his approval and signatures. Neel walked in precise footsteps to his chamber, greeted by his subordinate men. The file was placed under the nose of Neel for his signature. Neel swiftly opened the file and went through it entirely. The forged papers were so thin that they stuck to the thick bond authentic papers making them invisible. The papers were signed finally and the subordinate quickly snatched the file form Neel's prying eyes and went away.

At home a war was stirring up. Neel's children just got hold of a pair of roller skates and the younger one rode them all day. Weeks passed and one day the bell rang in the afternoon when the children had finished their lunch. Mala opened the door to find Mrs. Venkataswami,

'Sorry Mrs. Kumar but your children are a nuisance. The noise they make all day is deafening and is creating havoc in our lives. Me and my husband cannot bear the noise. Please do something or else we will lodge a formal complaint.'

'Well, I assure you, Mrs. Venkataswami, there will be no disturbance from now on. It is just that children will remain children. This is the time for play and fun. But I will ask them to leave the house and go elsewhere with those skates.'

Mrs. Venkataswami turned around in disgust and walked home ranting. After a few days the noise did not stop and Mala just could not hold the children from skating. Going out with the skates was very difficult. She just distracted herself from the thought of Mrs. Venkataswami and waited for any further warnings. Sure, enough after a two weeks gap Mrs. Venkataswami rang the bell once more.

'Mrs. Kumar, your children are a menace. I cannot do anything when I hear that noise. My roof starts quivering the moment skates roll over it. I don't think you understood Mrs. Kumar, I said I may take action. And just to tell you that I am going to report this to a higher authority, and please don't forget that my husband is your husband's boss. Goodbye, Mrs. Kumar.'

Neel sometimes lost his cool at home over the boys and beat them the way he did.

'I've got monsters at home. They won't let me live peacefully. Well, I may have hypertension, if that means nothing to these rascals.'

Days passed in stress for the entire family. The children knew nothing about bosses and the way they behaved towards their subordinates. They just wanted the kick out of the roller skates.

December arrived. It was a tense time for the entire forces. It was the time for the annual report. Every officer fought a silent battle with themselves, trying to assess their own performance. G.C. Venkataswami was chirpy these days. He did not worry about his own progress report, for he knew he will never leave the place he has until retirement. Neel avoided his boss and did not talk much at home. They boys moved around quietly not knowing why Neel was so silent. That day Neel got up early in the morning and made his way to the mess. He finished a pack of cigarettes and some gin to go with it. There was no officer at the mess besides bearers. The annual report lay at his table before he entered his chamber. The salutes of his men went unnoticed as he made his way in. He sent every one out and sat in silence for a while. The fan air kicked up the cover of the file that held his fate. He had made many mistakes on the way, and his children had also become culprits, he knew nothing about the forged papers. Fifteen minutes went by while he hung in the air like dragonflies. No one disturbed him. He took a deep breath, like he would fall down from his chair. His trembling hands pushed the file open. What he saw sent a cold wave down his spine. The report read,

'Mr. Neel Kumar, one of the most efficient and honest officers we have with us. I strongly recommend him for further promotion. His performance over the last year and many years before has been exemplary. I have absolutely no complaints against him. He is a model for all young officers, a backbone of our forces. I have never found such an honest officer. Well done, Sq. Ldr. Neel Kumar, you have passed the test and won the hearts of many.'

Neel had tears in his eyes and for a man who never showed his tears to anyone, not even to himself, his cried with all his heart and his whole. The files collected the sadness and the pain of one man through the years making the ink to blot. Neel collected himself and went home to be with his family.

Soon Neel Kumar was promoted and offered a place at New Delhi as a Wing Commander.

It is yet another tale about how Neel retired soon after that prematurely. His work was etched in history within the department he served. For a man who could not become a fighter flying officer, yet served the Indian Air Force during war and did a lot more than the forces expected of him. The cover of dangerous missions, the saviour of young and poor officers that worked for him, the risk taker, the person who died many times in service, will never be forgotten. Life comes once, we play just once. Some dazzle like the graceful ballerina, like a star that shines just once, live like a lion and leave this place like one. Here's bowing down to such brave people, fulfilling God's desire.

# SHAKTIMAN

THE FORCE

God created buses for schools that covered many kilometres and stops to dock at schools. Parents wished they change their routes to pick up children from unmarked places. But the bus driver never cared for children, so ruthless with time, when missing the bus was not bizarre. The parents then overloaded their scooters and drove the kids for miles to school, getting late for office as a punishment. Jolly's school was twenty kilometres from home and his father Marion mad sure the children were on the bus before it left for school. Morning time was a rush to get the children ready for school and dropping them at the bus stop. Jolly's elder brother Molly was very punctual and Marion didn't have to tell him what to do on those rush mornings. Marion barely finished his tea when every tick of the clock was like the slap of the morning siren asking the soldiers to assemble in the field. Marion was relaxed once the monsters disappeared while he finished the remaining tea in his cup. Marion had completed three years at the Allahabad Air Force Station and knew that his transfer was due. He was scared of being posted to extreme north, where the weather was inhospitable, too cold and dreary. His children were very young and they would find it hard to bear the extreme weather conditions. It was a given that when he got settled at a place of transfer, started loving the place with all its amenities and crowd, he was invariably thrown out of that place. So, when such feelings began to sink deep into him, he knew it was time to fly away.

The fear of transfer came true when one fine day at the officer's mess one of his seniors casually passed on the news of his new posting. That night Marion felt as if he were on a running train or a truck with his belongings due for a new destination. He was curious as to where he had been ordered to go. Morning came with heavy eyes as he lazily dropped the children to their bus stop and walked back like a drunken man. At his office he received the letter of his transfer. He had to head to Jalandhar, in the Punjab.

'Good heavens, it's so far away. How will my wife and children cope with such cold weather. I knew this was going to happen. Poor me.'

Marion remembered how twenty years ago, as a young cadet he had been stationed at Jalandhar Air Force Station. He was newly commissioned and the men under him loved the young officer. Back in Allahabad he and his family bid goodbye to friends and workers before embarking on a long journey north. Curiously their luggage and belongings were carried by Shaktiman, the three tonner. It rode all the way from Allahabad to Jalandhar without being noticed by the family travelling on a train. This was a sturdy truck, with thick canvas rolled around its top and sides at the back and a sound befitting a brave lion. The front bonnet was like a huge nose of the lion and the wheels big, rolling in grace. The nose had a print of red carrying its name.

The train arrived at the Jalandhar railway station at about two in the afternoon. As it entered the dome of the railway station loud noises erupted from nowhere of vendors, coolies shouting at the top of their voice. Hundreds of passengers running around with heavy loads with the train as it gave out its last whistle, coming to a halt. Marion was apprehensive about getting off the train with wife and kids and no one to receive them. He had no contacts and for a moment he felt his transfer was forced on him without his consent. There was no time to think as the train stationed itself by the side of the platform and people pushed each other indiscriminately to get out. The ones on the platform forced their way in simultaneously and Marion just lost his temper. He pushed hard with his luggage to make room for wife and kids. Bad words were exchanged and people just didn't have time to notice who said what. After a great struggle the family of four managed to get on the platform and Marion wiped the sweat from his face and combed his hair with a pocket comb he always carried. He urged his family to rest for a while and get some hot tea into their system while he thinks about what to do. Fifteen minutes went by and the family was ready to move. Marion knew exactly what to do, for he remembered how he got to the Air Force station as a young cadet twenty years ago. Just then a old sardar with a white beard and a dull purple turban came near Marion and said,

'Is that sahib? I am Airman Joginder Bhalla reporting, is that Sq. Ldr. Marion?'

Marion was quiet for a while and hastily replied,

'I am sorry, I don't quite recognize you, this must be a mistake.'

'Sir, please remember twenty years ago on that night when it was raining heavily. My mother was sick, very sick. She was on her death bed and needed an urgent operation. Do you remember how you immediately gave your costly watch and whatever money you had and rushed with me to the bus stop. It was raining sir, and you got all wet. You gave me an unwarranted sick leave of three weeks. Do you remember anything at all, sir. Well, my mother was saved, you are quite unaware of it, it seems. Do you remember how you helped all those airmen and 'khalasis' that worked under you giving them hidden leaves and a constant ear to hundreds of grievances. How can you forget, sir. I am seeing you after twenty years but we have never forgotten about you at all, sir. We talk about you and we were thrilled to hear that you are coming here, welcome sir.'

'I clearly remember Joginderji, I didn't want to be a burden on you.'

'Please never say that, let's go sir, our jeep is waiting outside. And just to inform you that your luggage has already reached the Air Force Station on a Shaktiman.'

Marion, an ordinary man, living an ordinary life, with a big heart. He had done deeds that even he did not remember.

The lunch was rich and delightful at the Air Force Mess, Jalandhar. Marion had never imagined such kind of welcome. He had learnt in life that he must carry his own luggage and provide for his family and himself, without anybody's help. Shaktiman stood gracefully outside the Mess doors, like the miles meant nothing to the three tonner.

Jolly and Molly were meant for schools that were far flung, a constant worry for Marion. This time the Air Force had set up a Shaktiman to travel twenty kilometres to Vajra Army School. They were to pick up kids on the way that were civilians. Shaktiman was most unfit for the long journey when the school children did not have the comforts of a bus. There were no seats within the truck and children were asked to hold the steel frame and pretend to sit with a slight bend of the back. The hands were not enough to grip the steel railings and very often them was a mass fall towards the pilot dome. The truck driver was very punctual and left the bus stop at five minutes past five in the morning. It was a big hurdle to cross each morning as the kids had to wake up at about four in the morning. The place was very cold and had below zero temperatures in the morning. Call it grace of God, or the thrust of parents, that Jolly and Molly never missed the bus in the morning. The biggest test for Jolly was getting into the truck. He was not more than four feet high and invariably he needed someone's hand to pull him into the truck with a floor that was more than four feet high. There were times when the truck moved without him inside and brought to a halt when he yelled out loud to pull him in. The Shaktiman travelled through villages and more villages on its long and bumpy ride. A sweet Punjabi girl got into the truck mid-way through the journey. She belonged to a village called Jhandu Singha, tall, oily hair tied up in two long ponytails ending in a bright red ribbon. Her face was always glowing and her smile was quite evident, and her spirits touching the skies. She did not need anyone's help to climb into the truck and very often she refused the hand that wanted to help her in. She looked around in a crisp white shirt and a long blue frock. Her fair skin added to her beauty and all boys turned their gaze on her when she jumped onto the floor. Jolly and Molly faced great difficulties when they had to wait for two hours after school for the Shaktiman to take them home. All the children slowly made their way out of the school gate while Jolly and Molly were left with no one in the campus. There were a few more kids with the same plight, waiting for the same Shaktiman. Some were older than Jolly and he would often get into a tussle with them in a game of basketball. Jolly could hardly shoot the ball into the basket, his reach was farther than most of the other boys. When the truck arrived, the boys were relieved and many would doze off in the way back. Some of the boys that were much older to Jolly stuck their head out in the front through the gap in the canvas just for fun. Their ties fluttered like in a great storm and sometimes a few even lost their glasses as it flew away from their eyes. The Shaktiman sometimes had a hole in the canvas that served as a window for the boys.

Jolly loved the school band and wanted to be a part of it. The bagpipers, trumpet, clarinet, drums, trombone were magical and elicited a kind of pride and the right way to live a life. Jolly especially liked the drum that was tied around the shoulders and placed on the thighs as the hands with sticks struck on it with a sweet rhythm while being pushed forward in marching steps. Therein came the nemesis for Jolly, a young lad named Jassi. Jassi was a stylish fair boy, tall and impressive, short hair and a great prankster. Unfortunately for Jolly he was a part of the school band and played the drums. Jolly had seen him in a lot of parades when Jassi, the lady killer marched in great confidence pushing the drum like a baby and had a sweet timing and coordination of the sticks in his hands and his accurate lunge forward. He was so used to playing the drum with finesse that he often stared at Jolly while effortlessly moving forward in a march. Jassi loved to play around with Jolly, the baby, and tease him until Jolly almost wept. Jolly tried to escape the eyes of Jassi but after school when Jassi too was a waiting member of the great big Shaktiman, he could hardly escape the eyes of the fox, the great Jassi. Jassi was hard to handle, because he was much taller and stronger, and he often managed to entangle Jolly in a deluge of obnoxious questions that were hard to answer and very often were aimed at irritating Jolly. Jolly had the drums in his mind though he knew that he was too short for the band and the drum would feel like a monster if he were to carry it. Besides Jolly was a simple, shy boy and could never even mention his love of the drums to anyone, not even Molly. Jassi the great bully never could play around and harass other boys for there was not a foolish, gullible, below average boy like Jolly. Jassi's smirk and his comments dented the confidence of Jolly, which he believed he had none, falling from the cliff of a dominating father. In any adverse interaction there is always a peak when things get out of control and people are hurt badly. Jassi was not happy with petty exchanges with Jolly that lasted no more than a few minutes and both parties forgot about it too soon.

It was the games period for the boys of the fifth grade, C section, of Vajra Army school. The boys entered a huge field and soon teams were made instantly for a game of football. Jolly was a part of the fifth-grade team. The other team was of the eighth grade with boys that had longer legs as compared to the other team. Jassi, out of nowhere, appeared as a part of the eighth-grade team. He spotted Jolly in no time. Jolly never saw more than the earth around him, being a shy, introvert and a low confidence and low esteem boy. He did not see Jass at all. Jolly was not a good player at all, all he knew that he could dribble the ball endlessly until he was injured and fell to the ground. Hence, he was placed at the back to counter a forward attack by the opposition. Jassi was the hero of the class, the captain, like a king. He was at the forward position to take the ball into the dee of the opposition and spank a certain goal. It happened in the second half of play. Jassi in the forward position came into action. A lone man in action moving forward like a storm. Nobody from the opposition came near him. They would rather leave him alone to score a goal than mess with his legs. Only Jolly, the fool came forward and tried to do the unthinkable. He ran to the ball held in control of the master. He dribbled hard, leaning to his left and falling down to be bathed in mud, getting up, leaning to the right and falling again and up again. Jassi started swearing at Jolly, using words that were most unlike young boys. Jolly had deep cuts on his legs and hands, while Jassi fought more with dirty words than his legs, knowing that a less than four-foot boy could not afford much. Jolly fell too many times, yet never gave up the dual. Jassi was enraged, he gently called the boy and with a right kick which carried all his strength hit the ball very hard. The ball hit Jolly on the face, he got blinded and there was blood around his temples and lips. Jolly could not carry on while there were shouts of victory as Jassi had scored the final goal. Jassi ran away from the scene and tried to hide. Jolly was carried to the medical room in the room and given treatment.

Days later Molly tried to confront Jassi and fight the tall lad. Molly could not do much and from that day Jassi stayed away from

Jolly and did not say a word to him. He was scared of Jolly reporting the matter to the principal. Each day after school Jolly and Jassi sat on two opposite corners of the Shaktiman and never looked at each other.

It was a Friday. All children were looking bright and cheerful, wanting to finish off the day soon and enjoy the weekend. Jolly was happy too. He had forgotten about what happened in the football field. The classes were negotiated at ease as Jolly and Molly patiently waited for the Shaktiman to arrive after school hours. Jassi was nowhere to be seen. Jolly played basketball with one eye on the road waiting for the arrival of the truck. He knew the fact that on Saturday his mother prepared some delightful dishes and offered him cakes and ice creams. Hours passed like an unfelt breeze and finally the boys were packed into the truck and the final hook was stuck hard into the slot to hold the back flap firmly. The driver was given a go signal by someone slapping the steel hard with hands. The driver shifted the gear and truck started moving. It had travelled about fifty metres when Jolly saw a hand far away, as if trying to stop the truck. It was a young lad running diagonally off the truck which no one could see. The truck picked up speed and it was certain that it would not stop for anything. The boy was parting in the distance and slowing down a wee bit, very sure he had missed it. Jolly yelled with all his strength and banged the steel rails with hands hurting his soft hands. The driver would not listen. He looked at Molly and the two shouted with all the air in their lungs. The sudden noise fell like lightning on the driver's ears and he suddenly pulled up. The lad started running even harder until he reached the truck, panting. The back flap was unhooked and Jolly gave a hand to the white lad, looking into the eyes of Jassi. Jassi was pulled in and he gave a warm hug to Jolly. He had tears in his eyes,

'I am so sorry, my friend. If I had missed this truck then you don't know what could have happened. My house is more than thirty-five kilometres from here. My parents are waiting for me, we go to the Gurudwara every Saturday. You have saved me. I am a kid and can never reach home without this Shaktiman. We are friends for life, I shall never hurt you. You see, every creation of God has an important place in this world, we all are invaluable, no one is worthless. We must respect every creation and not be lost in ourselves and the huge castle of our ego. Thank you again, my friend, I have never seen anyone like you.'

Jolly's dream of getting into the band never came true. Jassi knew all about it and just said,

'You'll play your own drums one day, that will be the loudest in the world to hear.'

# SCHOOL BUNK

TRUE SCHOOL

All so famous names in this world have bunked school. It is not a crime for them for God has always rewarded them with more than what they have wished. As time passed school bunk became a symbol of protest to the nonsense that is 'school'. Not surprising then is to observe that sporadic school bunks leading to a complete drop of school has given us great men and women of this world. If life is nothing but a singular scheme to amass wealth and a big name, then the stupid school hours are nothing but a waste of time. Twenty years of schooling, as they say, and you are not capable enough for a job. It is also true that man has never wanted more than an end to the curse called poverty. A simple business man on the streets selling sweetmeat or some spicy concoction earns more than an unemployed man who has spent twelve years in school followed by another four to five years in a degree course. This is not a philosophy lesson but the story of a little boy called Sagar that committed the crime of bunking school.

St. Marks was an all-boys school situated on the outskirts of the city of Kandar. It was a Christian school run by cassock clad Fathers. It was the best school in the city. It had a huge playground that was filled with children during lunch hours. The rest of the time it looked sad and pensive with not even a bird on its chest. When the children arrived, so did eagles and vultures filling up the skies that changed its dress frequently. The eagles flew in hoards, low, with eyes pinned on sumptuous tiffin boxes in innocent hands. When the target was decided, the eagles dived into the hands of little boys, grabbed food with both hands and looped high into the skies, leaving behind numb hands and senses. The vultures on the other hand looked for dead meat and surprisingly only appeared during the lunch hours. There were some great men and women 'to-be' among the crowd but also foolish ones like Sagar. Sagar had a strict father, Ramesh, who was in the Army, and his word was like the final word from heaven. Ramesh kept a close eye on his two boys, Sagar and Vikas, Sagar being the younger one. Ramesh had outlived the dazzle and the good days of marriage, especially the honeymoon and now life was a big burden for him. There was nothing left between him and his wife Radha. It was much like the school that is thrust on every child, albeit with a difference. This was the school of 'life' and there was no possibility in India to quit this school. The same principle perhaps applied to the drop of marriage, or 'divorce' if someone wanted something different from life. Ramesh sometimes was so disgusted with his life that he spoke his mind openly to his wife and children that he was planning to leave them all and run away forever. The children could not understand why he said so and Sagar was the one crying like it were all over. Ramesh was a mature man in his late thirties and certainly did not understand why he had been made to live a life that was a burden from the start. Everyday was struggle in the office and home turned out to be a place where he could not find peace. But a marriage in India is forever and the couple are bound to fade away carrying the burden of children on their shoulders. All Ramesh could look forward to was his children. The struggle of Radha and Ramesh was for the children alone. Ramesh kept the fire on the stove burning while Radha made sure that her children had enough to eat. Every parent, at least in India, put their entire life at stake and burnt for their children, sometimes forsaking their evenings of pleasure with friends and allowing a holiday during the annual break of the school of their children. As fate would have it, very few children, if not none at all, become the eyes of their parents when they tire and become weak as in old age.

Sagar had no plans for the future. All he ever wanted was to attend classes at school and redress his shortcomings and the stigma of being below average. He just managed to elicit a short word written without enthusiasm sometimes aversion, 'Promoted'. At the time of the distribution of report cards, Ramesh was called by the class teacher of Sagar's class. She looked into the eyes of Ramesh and said,

"Sir, your son is not working hard enough. I don't see any improvement in this child at all. If he does not bring about changes in his performance, he is going to find it hard to survive in higher classes. Here is the report card, thank you for coming."

Ramesh took a quick look at the yellow report card, kicked the scooter hard and asked Sagar to jump in,

"You have been promoted, Sagar. Well done, let's go home and we will pick some of your favourite samosas on the way. That's right, c'mon let's do it."

Ramesh had no signs of remorse or regret for he knew that Sagar was honest and true and this was no age to worry about anything.

This was the life in its entirety for Ramesh and Radha, their two sons, that brought joy on their faces.

It was a Saturday and the school had a half day. Boys wore casual dresses and no one was in the mood for any books. They had all planned their weekend in advance with friends and family. Sagar and Vikas hopped into the school bus as if it were the last day at school. It was going to be a three-period day and the children could go home after that. Sagar had English, Hindi and the final Mathematics class. Sagar and Vikas didn't have many friends in the bus and Sagar especially was like a pawn, short and indistinct, a follower of hefty bullies. Vikas belonged to the senior section and the school bus did not have many boys of his age group. They were mostly the age of Sagar and thereabouts. Vikas sat at the back of the bus, alone while Sagar was always a part of a group that thrived on short and gullible people like him. The weather was nice and cloudy with the wind blowing in a hundred directions. The voices of the boys were drowned by the noise of the moving bus, the garrulous wind and the horn of the bus that had no boundaries this fun day. The only thing that could be heard was the laughter of the boys when the leader among them cracked a joke and the ponies like Sagar had to laugh even louder without hearing a word spoken by the boss. Such days were rare and it felt as if the entire city was on a picnic, singing and dancing. Even the bus driver whistled a tune and the conductor provided the orchestra of fingers on the metal bonnet. People in the bus were on a high and this usually led to something outrageous to the extent of breaking the rules. The children ran down the steps of the bus as it stopped at the school gate. Vikas was the last one to get off with a hanging head as if it were a dead Monday. Sagar was lost among the boys trying to keep up with the tall lads and telling himself that he was also a part of the group even though he was never considered one among them. The boys instead of walking to the classroom gathered under a tree near the water tank and Sagar was invited too. Sagar walked with pride feeling like a special person and did not understand why all eyes went to him for a moment with a soft beckon round their shoulders. Sagar was too happy and spread his hands ducking in a huddle among the boys.

"Boys, we have gathered here to bunk classes. There is a one-day international match being held in the stadium not far from here and I have heard that Sunil Gavaskar and Kapil Dev are also going to come. Let's not miss this golden opportunity, boys, let go straight to the stadium, we have to arrange the tickets too. Come on everyone, empty your pockets, this is a once in a lifetime opportunity."

Sagar was dumbfounded. He had never bunked classes in his entire school going days. Somewhere inside him he knew that bunking classes is a sin. It is as bad as cheating one's parents. He also did not want to miss the chance to be a member of the elite group of bullies that also were the most popular lads in the school. He wanted to help the boys and become a prominent figure in the gang and so far, he had spent his life like a dumb ass and his physique was far from daunting. He had walked alone always and his spoken words did not ever elicit any kind of attention or curiosity. He had been non existent so far and for the first time the boys wanted something from him. He could not deny such glances and if bunking school could help his plight then so be it.

Five boys including Sagar decided to bunk school that Saturday. Luckily Sagar had a fifty rupee note which Ramesh had given his son for those orange flavour ice creams that had a hidden milky bar within. Ramesh had quietly handed over the note just before Sagar got into the bus with a belated wink. When the leader presented the palm of his hands, the boys emptied their pockets one by one and placed whatever they had. Sagar was the last one to present a crackling fifty rupee note and all were impressed as they wowed his share that was a lot more than some of the others. The boys were to take a ride on a tempo that had an aggravated nose of an engine like someone's nose had been bitten by a nasty bee. The ride would take them around the main city centre, into the small lanes and finally the huge stadium on the edge of the city. There was no problem so far with the finances and the boys did not lose the puffed-up cheeks of excitement and fun while the tempo fired cannon balls in the air. Sagar's thought sometimes went to the empty seat in his class and the red mark in the attendance register against his name when he had actually been to school that Saturday.

Five boys could not travel together; hence two tempos were hired. Invariably one tempo got totally cut off from the other tempo. Boys sometimes grew anxious when such a thing happened. The leader then stepped in and demonstrated a fake sense of patience to calm the boys but the boys in the tempo without him were scared to death. The trial lasted for more than one hour until finally the huge stadium put some life back into the boys. Luckily all the five boys arrived intact at the stadium and held hands like that huddle in school. Everyone had a smile on their lips and Sagar just loved the attention of grown-up boys. There was a huge crowd trying to enter the stadium and the boys had no clue how to cut through the mayhem. The leader summoned everyone under a huge shady tree that had a cement pedestal.

"Alright friends, this is the time for action. Please hold each other's hands while entering the stadium. How much have we got. Let's see, a hundred, one more hundred and finally a fifty, which makes a total of two hundred and fifty rupees. The cost of each ticket in the back row is rupees one hundred, which makes the total cash required as five hundred. We have only two hundred and fifty, which is half the fare. And we are doomed, my friends. Good news is that we have enough money to get back to school, which I think is the best alternative under the given conditions. Anyone has any other idea, please let us know."

All the boys hung their head in disgrace. The leader was the smartest among the lot and could not bear the helplessness in the eyes of the boys.

"But, but I have a plan. And I hope it works. You see the huge crowd my friends. We will take advantage of the mayhem and with only two and half tickets we shall watch our dream teams. All we have to do is form a straight chain among the boys, the top two boys will hold the ticket and enter the stadium while the remaining three, which includes me will push our way through and enter without tickets. The crowd is so thick that just the one ticket collector is not enough to check every spectator. I have experience boys; we shall make it. C'mon now don't sit and cry. Be a man."

The tickets were promptly purchased and as luck would have it Sagar was the last boy in the chain. His entry was the toughest and being slight in design he was bound to be caught. The leader was smart, he placed himself the third in the chain just to show solidarity. The third was highly likely to get in given his size and the momentum that the top two boys created. Sagar for a moment wanted to withdraw and head towards school, not being sure of getting in. But it was too late now, the boys had already formed a chain and the top two boys had presented their tickets to the ticket collector. The top two boys ran as fast as they could and forced their way in as if they were ticketless. The momentum they created was so huge that Sagar didn't know when and how he had entered the stadium and quietly occupied a seat at the back row. The leader was so happy, he passed on paper caps to all the boys and gave a high five to all, including Sagar. The boys were elated. They had succeeded in their plan and all the credit went to the leader.

Half an hour passed without even looking at the match that was going on. Someone said,

"Look that's Ashok Malhotra batting."

The leader was confused and asked a fellow spectator about the match.

"Don't you know, this a Ranji trophy match, we have all come to see Ashok Malhotra in his full gear."

"Good heavens, this is a Ranji trophy match. Boys there is no Sunil Gavaskar or Kapil Dev. We have been cheated."

Sagar never felt cheated. He enjoyed the match. It was a great fortune to see a serious cricket match with a running commentary and the great Ashok Malhotra.

The boys were happy in spite of the error of judgement and pop corn baskets were the order of the day. Sagar was happy to be passed on a huge basket of popcorn by one of the big boys and he felt he had suddenly matured. The match went on for two more hours before lunch time. The boys decided to return to school during the lunch break. Since it was a half day the school had broken off at sharp twelve noon. It was half past two now and Sagar suddenly started sweating in nervousness. The school bus must have reached home by now while he was not even at school. The boys were happy to have succeeded in what they had intended. They all got into a single jumbo tempo that shot its way to school. There was enough money left in the leader's pocket to pay for the fare of five boys. He wondered how and why all the other boys were so happy, didn't they know that they had missed the bus. Such thoughts and some more taking him to the scary eyes of his father especially when he would realize that Sagar had played truant to school. The light weather was still in full swing inviting men and women to come of their houses and plan a picnic. The wind was reckless to the point of insanity but it only gave cold sweats to Sagar. The tempo stopped and the boys pushed Sagar out of his long stretch of seriousness and alighted the tempo. That was the last point of brotherhood and civility after which four boys disappeared into four different directions like they had never met. Sagar was left cold and before he could cry out for help, he was left alone. Sagar wanted to cry but the busy streets and the normal chaos did not allow him to shed his tears. There was no money in his pocket and there was no way he could get home. It was evening time and the sky got darker. He walked from the bus stop around the huge school playground and finally to the main gate of the school. He decided to walk to the office but did not have the courage to ask someone for help. For once he thought he had lost his family and would never see the faces of Papa and Muma again. He sat down on the cemented bricks of the pavement like little lost children do. His hands and arms were cold and with hands on his knees he stooped low to cover his head. It was getting darker and the street lights had been turned on. For once he broke down and cried aloud with his body trembling under his sobs. A man in a faded helmet ran to him and picked him up as he buried his face in that man's chest. He raised his eyes in despair to find that it was the chest of Ramesh.

"Poor baby, what happened to you. Why are you alone, what happened, please don't cry. I am here and will take you home on my scooter. Don't worry, I am with you."

That long ride home had Sagar on the pillion with his arms around the waist of Papa and his eyes pointing into his Papa's back, far away from the cruel world. It was as if centuries passed by in total peace and calm. He was helped by Ramesh home and Sagar never opened his eyes until he lay on Papa's bed. Sagar was offered some hot Bournvita by Muma and every member was in that small room. Sagar began the saga with his head buried low on the bed as if he had committed a great sin. Papa, Muma and Vikas listened very carefully. Ramesh got up before the end and interrupted Sagar,

"Good heavens, you bunked school, so what. It's OK. My God you have great courage, I must say. You planned a trip to the stadium with the boys, I mean that's like my son. Stop crying son, you have done something that I am proud of, not the bunking part, but the part where you went to the stadium all alone, without dada. You are not the kind that will bunk school, remember that. For you obeying your elders is the greatest virtue, even if it takes you nowhere. You know how to keep promises, and that is a rare kind. Cheer up! Now, and I shall get your favourite samosas tonight. Come listen to some music, you'll be fine."

Sagar was filled with gratitude and it made him a stronger person. He vowed never to bunk school again, especially because it was a gift from his loving parents. He resolved to keep promises and if need be, die for them. He felt it was more important to look into himself and correct the faults within and not point fingers at people who desired something off him.

# THAT FORLORN LADY

FORLORN LADY

Our family of four moved into New Delhi, my father's last posting before retirement from The Indian Air Force. My father served the forces for twenty-one years which included superseding some high rank officers to become a Wing Commander. Adept at his work he was known to complete twenty-eight years of work in his twenty-one years of service. Quite a remarkable man and an astounding career meant that his two children could not inherit his hard work and dedication to the point of a rare genius. But my father had other plans. Everyone around including a huge family of relatives had the obvious question on their minds,

"Why are you taking a premature retirement, especially when your children are growing up and would need quality education. Why in the world are you returning home to Patna after retirement, which is the dirtiest place known to humanity."

My father gave health reasons for such a drastic change in environment and that essential hypertension requires a regular monitor by doctors and ample rest. Yet he softly whispered to himself the real reason for such a decision.

"I am doing it for the boys."

This event however was imminent after one full year, during which the boys attended the Air Force school and he reported to the Western Air Command, New Delhi.

Life at Saket, New Delhi was a small house with two bedrooms, a dining room, kitchen and a drawing room. There was a porch, a small garden and a white off-colour gate with a tree of white flowers with yellow shades at the meeting point of the generous petals. Their undoing was their delicate fragrance and the flowers bloomed once again after their indifferent plucking. My father was an optimist deep down and would flood the children's ambience with books and more books. Most of them were beyond the children and would never be touched. Yet he would spend some time each day for his children's progress, being absent from his office during the working hours. He brought them a guitar, a tuition teacher to get them interested in books and the obvious tonic of books and some more books. Being a man of understanding and wisdom, he had reached a great height of accomplishment and a leader at his office. Even his seniors came to him for advice in serious matters and very often would place him in important conferences where delegates worldwide wanted to hear something meaningful. Sometimes in a quiet moment he tried to search for the reason why he was still alive. Certainly not for his wife that had outlived her life and now it was just like being trapped with a lady in a house. His parents were not alive and he was not close enough to any of his relatives, nor did he have any childhood friends. The argument rested on his two sons and he did not know why he found some hope in them, although doing something worthwhile in a life is an impossible task, especially for the new generation.

My mother was a devoted housewife. She had chosen the house above everything else. A simple lady, she did not have the sophistication of those urban women that lived on their tongue of some popular English words that were in vogue with latent silence over vowels. She did not carry expensive stuff that other ladies did to illustrate their high class. Yet she carried the voice and the heart that could beat the most accomplished ladies of the west. What fell in between was utter garbage. My mother was fond of flowers and trees and the only one we had at the entrance was her immediate concern. Once on a sunny afternoon she happened to take a walk in the lawn with a cup in her hands. Suddenly her eyes fell on a lady on the third floor of the adjoining building. The lady almost past her middle age smiled at my mother. My mother had a very soft nature and was friendly towards anyone she met.

"Hello, I am Mrs. Srivastava. I have seen you often on the balcony of your house."

"Nice to meet you. I am Mrs. Divan and we have been living here for about ten years now."\

"Please come for tea, whenever you can."

"Sure, Mrs. Srivastava."

Days passed without a sound like it is in a big city. My father was in and out with precision and us two brothers looked for ways to enjoy and have fun, like kids do. A chocolate bar to me was more exciting than sitting inside a classroom and running to and fro at the random sound of bells. My parents often had meetings over cups of tea when they would discuss something important especially concerning the nagging nature of relatives. My father was the eldest in his family and his younger brothers and sisters would follow him and ask him to arrange their trip to New Delhi. They wanted to shop at Connaught Place and Palika Bazaar, go around to visit monuments like the Qutub Minar or the majestic India Gate, Lotus Temple, Humayun's Tomb, etc. My relatives on my mother's side wanted to visit Agra for the Taj Mahal and my father often made an authentic excuse of being too busy with work. My father often said,

"I know New Delhi like the back of my hand. I can tell you exactly where you are and the route to any corner of New Delhi."

It is quite funny that my father never took us anywhere. We were either in the school or in the house or in the park next to our house.

One morning quite unexpectedly the door bell rang. My mother was alone in the house. She opened the door to find her neighbour Mrs. Divan.

"Hello Mrs. Srivastava. I had nothing much to do this morning and so I thought why not visit your house. I hope I am not disturbing you."

"Absolutely not. Please come in Mrs. Divan. I was thinking of visiting you myself but you know how it is with family affairs. There's just no room for anything."

The two ladies sat down in the drawing room and mother prepared some hot tea, served with some coconut cookies. There was silence in the air when the two ladies sat down with the tea and biscuits, like out of lines to say anything. Mrs. Divan began with hesitation.

"I am probably much older than you. I have two grown up sons and my husband passed away about two years ago. My bahu(daughter-in-law) is here with me. My elder bahu stays with my elder son about thirty kilometres from here. This is the wife of my younger son. She also sometimes has to leave for a few days on some urgent business. I love my family, especially my two sons. I saw you shift here, what is it, two years ago, am I right?"

"I am sorry Mrs. Divan for not visiting you earlier. Yes, we moved in here about two years ago. My home is in Bihar and my husband's last posting was in Bamrauli, Allahabad, the Central Air Command. I have two sons; one is eleven years old and the elder one is thirteen years old. We find this place very strange; I am sorry for saying so. Back in Allahabad there was a close community feeling and friends met on a regular basis. Here I find that the culture of having neighbours as friends does not exist. Each one, I find is living on an island of his own. It's not the first time we have lived in New Delhi, mind you. My husband's second posting of his career was in Shahjahan Road, New Delhi. I find that this place has rapidly deteriorated. Imagine you have been with us for two years and this is the first time we have met. I am sorry for being so critical to the extent of being obnoxious, perhaps."

"Mrs. Srivastava, please don't be sorry. There's no excuse for people if they forget that they are a part of a society and being social is what makes a human species."

The two ladies soon found a common ground in art. If nothing else my mother spent her free time in crating artwork- like making jute curtains by braiding, crochet work, knitting, making designs on cloth by artistic needlework, making drawing on charcoal, patch work, and some more. Luckily Mrs. Divan struck a common chord with my mother. She was one step ahead of my mother. After a little while the two ladies got comfortable with one another, especially carrying similar views on everyday life and the perhaps the greatest quality that each woman shared- a sense of humility. By the looks of it, Mrs. Divan hardly ever opened her mouth and a smile was a counter reply in all situations. It was like someone that had lived an entire life which carried a bulk of bitter experiences, had decided finally to present a shut mouth in any given situation and it was hard to elicit anything except a smile. Such people realize after years and years of suffering and torture that words are of no value at all.

But Mrs. Divan somehow opened up to my mother, a very rare occurrence, like my mother held the key to the rest of her life. Her eyes squinted and a funny kind of smile erupted on her face. Her cheeks were finally visible which were like two hot air red balloons. Her insides were yelling out to her,

"Where have you been, so far."

And then there was the lack of time. The ladies had duties to perform and it was as if Mr. Divan was out of the door but still hanging on to a precious discussion. My mother got excited when someone her ken was sitting before her and then she hit the tea pot rather hard, not wanting the exchange to ever end. My mother remembered her Air Force days in Allahabad where there were a couple of ladies like Mrs. Divan turned out to be.

"I better be going Mrs. Srivastava. Remember I am just an arm's length away from you and so please don't mind my butting in without any notice. I have to show you some of my paintings, it seems, my God, Mrs. Srivastava, you have made my day. Bye now."

Mother was fully charged with two pots of tea but there was still time for her husband and children to reach home.

We all noticed a change in my mother from that day. Gone were the days when my mother would just run through the day like the sun and the moon doing their rounds over and over again. She was chirpy, playing games with us children, cracking jokes in her peculiar smile, preparing some unusual colourful dishes and the best of them all was her laughter- when my mother laughed aloud, the whole neighbourhood could hear it and the walls shook like some kind of tremor. Perhaps I got her laughter and in my later years when I grew up and got a job, my bosses would stop me by my shoulder and requested,

"Please laugh for me once."

My mother was so excited that she performed all her duty to perfection and waited with bated breath for her next meeting with Mrs. Divan. This is a natural trait of all womenfolk, perhaps; all they want is to talk to someone and pour out all that they hold.

The next time came soon. It was Saturday morning and the ladies had already fixed a meeting through telephone. Mrs. Divan arrived at nine in the morning when we were at school and my father at work. Mrs. Divan carried a stack of cloth pieces in her hand. There was the tea pot hot and ready, two cups with saucers and some hot samosas this time. Without a word Mrs. Divan picked one cloth piece at a time from the stack and presented them to my mother. There was a peacock with a painted head and neck, its feathers had been sown out of colourful thread, so was its beak and painted legs. Mrs. Divan kept showing the cloth pieces that had beautiful paintings of birds, flowers, partly painted and partly in woven thread. My mother was amazed but maintained silence until Mrs. Divan reached the last piece of cloth.

"Mrs. Divan this is astounding. I am not a painter at all, but mam, what a talent. It tells me all about you, Mrs. Divan. Such perfection and beauty come from years of suffering and sacrifice and the great value of truth in your life. Mam, I myself do not easily make friends because I feel that most women belong to the rotten lot where an easy road is the one that is sought without hesitation or qualms of righteousness."

Mrs. Divan was quiet. She drank the tea while my mother poured herself on her guest like she usually did when she found someone right to talk to. There were tales and tales and it made Mrs. Divan come out her sadness in no time. Mrs. Divan also narrated stories from her long life and at my mother's request promised to teach my mother basics of painting including an introduction to oil paints and the different kind of brushes used in painting.

Mrs. Divan left with a promise to come again soon. My mother imagined herself learning some new for of art like the hands on a brush which she had desired right from childhood. There was a Bengali painter babu that lived next to my mother's house. He spent his days before a canvas, with colours spilt on his white kurta and a wonderful wife. He had been cursed to make a living out of his paintings of which there were just a handful customers. My mother often ran to his window to watch him paint and sometimes walked into his room. But familial pressures and a strict mother that always wanted her with the boundaries of her home, she could go any further than a grip on the brush.

Mrs. Divan came very often and the two ladies opened up to each other a lot more, until,

"Mrs. Divan why are you so hesitant to talk about your family. But I like to say that I enjoy your company and I find you very humble and easy to talk to. I have started painting, yes, and the artist in me has suddenly awakened. I am never going to paint like you but I like the idea of painting along with thread work. It's so fascinating."

It was a Sunday. A great break for the family members from unending work. My father had made up his mind to get up late and us kids were on the same road. Mt mother too got up late, yet earlier than the men folk. It was a silent morning, just like we had expected.

At about half past eight there was a big noise that came crashing through our windows. It was from someone that was in deep pain. It was a strange noise that made my father and the children jump put of our beds. The children were scared and my father looked at my mother for some clues. Someone was crying at the top of their throat and my father rushed through the entrance to take a look. We too came out with my mother.

We found Mrs. Divan lying on the floor, crying in a lot of pain. When asked, we were told that Mrs. Divan had jumped from the third floor of her balcony. She wanted to end her life and my mother just could not understand why. There had been a long gap since the last visit of Mrs. Divan to our home and my mother had made up her mind to go to her place. But somehow the family duties were stopping her each time she made an effort to go to Mrs. Divan's house. Suddenly there was a huge SUV that parked itself near our house. Out came the two sons of Mrs. Divan and their wives. They took her away and went to the hospital to admit her and get her treated. My mother did not hear from Mrs. Divan for weeks. The house was locked and only the morning bird sat at the window sill as a guest for a few minutes. My mother lost all interest in painting and the idea of learning something new. She sat at a chair at night looking blankly into the air. But it could only last for half hour as the sound of duty came knocking and she had to do the needful.

About five weeks later a sad new came to our door. Mrs. Divan had passed away. She had left behind her house, two kids and their wives. My mother went into grief and she did not talk to anyone for days.

Mrs. Divan had tried to hide her sadness and anything about her family. Her two sons were IAS officers. They had left their mother alone and were too busy with their work. They did not spare time even on weekends to ask her how their mother was. The wives did not want an old and a sick woman in their lives. They showed no compassion, love or care for the old lady. The forlorn lady sat at her balcony all day without eating anything. My mother was a little spark in her life but was not enough to give her the desire to live and be happy. She often avoided talking about her family and even on being pushed towards some truth, she caved into her shell and preferred to remain silent. That attempt to commit suicide was the saddest event in our lives. We never forgot Mrs. Divan and the brutality of her sons. A sad tale for a woman that lived for her family and spread beauty through her artwork and humility. Time shall never forget and the evil shall have its due.

# TALENT AT TAFS

GREAT BOYS AND GIRLS

The record shows that my brother and me have had the opportunity to study in the best of schools around northern India. Thanks to my dear father who wanted to bring out the best in his children. He sent us to the most popular schools be it Bal Bharti, New Delhi, St. Joseph's College Allahabad, The Vajra Army school, Jalandhar, the Air Force school, Subroto Park, New Delhi, Don Bosco Academy, Patna and finally St. Michael's High school, Patna. Little did he know that no one spoke in English in these English medium schools, every one was an expert in swearing and cussing, boys looked down upon young girls including the young women who were teachers at our school, mass bunking was the norm, and finally chewing on tobacco and using the filthiest language possible was a tradition. The only bright spark in these schools was perhaps the subjects were all in English language and that is why it was an English medium school.

The Air Force school or TAFS for short is located in the picturesque location of Subroto Park New Delhi. This was perhaps because it was primarily an Air Force area where one of the headquarters of the Indian Air Force, the Western Air Command is located. My brother and me had never seen such a beautiful school in our lives. On one side there were rocks and offshoots of bamboo trees, as many as three massive playgrounds among which one was more a park than a playground, huge buildings for classes, a huge arts hall and so much more than a sentence can hold. I was in the sixth grade and my big brother in the ninth grade. I don't remember ever seeing him during school hours because we went to far away buildings. The impressive school and its majestic environment made us totally forget our homes for those seven or eight hours that we were away. Each morning was a struggle to get ready after a harsh wakeup call from parents. The bus was a local DTC bus, green and yellow in colour. The driver appeared to be playing a harp, the way he changed those far away gears and turned a huge steering wheel. We did miss the bus sometimes when we were plucked like a harsh hand plucks a flower, out of our beds and we arrived at the bus stop half asleep. My father was red with rage on such occasions as he mercilessly kicked his scooter to give us a ride. I was probably about eleven to twelve years old then and life became a lot more serious than before. People started noticing me and friends just walked into my life like they were in competition. My memory became a lot stronger and I could hold more facts in my head than ever before. Yet I was not old enough to be deprived of chocolates from my young aunts and a sweet kiss on my cheeks from their wet lips of red. And I had three beautiful young aunts, just for the record. I did not meet them very often because we did not travel much from New Delhi to Patna, my home town, where these aunts of mine were in that blushing period before marriage.

My class had just three girls- tall and thin Sonali, Archana with her curly short hair like a tied bunch of flowers, quite healthy and robust and the leader of the pack, Reva, tall, fat and huge, not fit to be in the sixth grade but she carried herself like a beauty, desired yet untouched. I did not fall in love with any of the girls and stayed away from them because they always occupied the exclusive front bench, right next to the teacher. They always sat together and I have no idea what they thought of the boys in the class. I may have had a short conversation with one of the girls, especially Sonali because she was less threatening, but it was too long ago for me to remember anything. All I knew was that these girls were very smart, just like big city girls. No one could pass a frivolous comment on them because they were bold enough to walk up to the principal and file a complaint in immaculate English. And as we all know that this age belongs to girls and women, and men should rather behave and not try to indulge in any cheap behavior. Reva, the tallest and strongest was the star of the class. Her English was a lesson to even the teachers that avoided situations that demanded an English tongue. I can never forget that morning when Reva took the mic in the morning assembly. I have never seen such courage and boldness in a student of the sixth grade. In a class of boys' majority, no one could speak the way Reva spoke that morning,

"Pope Zau-Pol...."

I don't remember anything else from her speech but only the way she spoke of the Pope John Paul II, the then head of the Catholic church. She spoke with authority and pride like a woman without fear and looking the dignitaries in the eye. I must tell you at that age of mine, I could not utter a word before a crowd and that was the reason why I avoided crowds and even when the teacher called out my name in a packed class, I tried to negotiate the matter in a few timid words. Was it something to do with the way I was brought up, yes indeed, my father was strict and roared like a lion and when he lost his temper, his eyes spit lightning that would numb my body. And so, we, my brother too was the prey, would rather keep quiet than mumble words that did not make any sense.

Every morning my brother and me would take the DTC bus to school. On the way I had to encounter an old foe, Paresh, who was also with us at Bamrauli Air Force station, Allahabad, where my father was posted, before transfer to New Delhi, as a Squadron Leader. This was a short boy but stung like a scorpion. Invariably I had to sit with him and even if I didn't, he would walk to my seat and show his face. He was a Mathematics wizard and I was glad that I could add simple numbers like one and two. He would throw mathematical puzzles at me just to show his prowess,

"You complete idiot, you can't solve such a simple puzzle. You dumbo, you'll go nowhere for this world can only be conquered through mathematics. Such an ass, OK here is a simpler one, just for you."

I probably now understand what he was trying to do. But back then, I felt like a complete idiot. I looked into his cunning eyes with shame and he was ready to pounce on me with his philosophy of life. Yes, a child of the sixth grade carries his own philosophy of life. I was glad of the fact that he was not in my section, although he too was of the sixth grade. I felt incomplete when I was before my father at home and with Paresh, when I was on my way to school. I never learnt pointing fingers at people, but saw myself lacking of so many things I ought to have, especially confidence and self-worth. I have struggled with these things almost all my life, but that is yet another story. There was one great advantage of my friendship with Paresh. Being a south Indian, he carried a tiffin and we often met during lunch break on the rocks that was lined with bamboo trees. I have never tasted such South Indian food in my entire life. The mysterious ingredient in all his dishes was the south Indian gun powder or Milagai Podi. I just snatched his tiffin as a recompense for all the shit he gave me in the bus and ate all his food of delicious idli, vada and chutney and tossed my tiffin of puri and subji to him. He just did not resist because he did not find such a fool anywhere that would tolerate his highbrow nonsense. He did not test me during the lunch break and I vividly remember a carpenter on one side peeling the flesh out of fresh wood. My search for a friend landed me with a black guy like me by the name of V. Bharat. I don't know how or when we became friends but I often moved around with him during lunch breaks or free periods and sat next to each other in the same class. The common trait among us was simplicity, room for convenient exchange of words and moments of complete silence when we just heard each other's breath. V. Bharat never tested me like Paresh did and his smile was warm and inviting. He listened to me and followed me and I did the same. I thanked the Lord when Paresh was absent from school for a day and I could engage with Bharat and vent my feelings casually. Even when Paresh came to school, I sometimes avoided him and fled with Bharat to some other place instead of the rocks. Our friendship grew stronger and we exchanged our tiffin very often. The star of our class was one called Vijay Arora. We had a class cricket team and Vijay Arora was an excellent batsman and bowler too. We played plastic ball cricket during lunch breaks with our tiffin boxes/free hand serving as a bat. Vijay Arora could hit the ball very hard and ran the fastest in the class. I was a willy-nilly player and sometimes hit a great shot which went unnoticed because it was too few and far between. There was another stout and stout guy by the name of Amit Vij. He was a great bowler, surprisingly, and a leader at par with Vijay Arora.

It is the funniest happening of my life, perhaps. I have never experienced such a thing ever in my life. I loved playing cricket with the boys and the top brass liked the way I put up a fight for everything. I have always struggled with my weight throughout my life. There was a time that I was coached by a former Ranji Trophy player from Bihar by the name of Prateek Narayan. He liked the way I batted and drew similarity with the legend Sunil Gavaskar. The reason for such a thought was that I could never hit a cricket ball. I always defended any ball thrown at me. But I was rejected and could not advance any further with cricketer because I was an overweight child with a paunch. Prateek Narayan asked me to quit cricket and never allowed me to participate in local matches. My brother however was lean and wiry and an excellent fast bowler. He was always invited to play matches not just because of his bowling but because, eighth down, he could hit the ball high in the air like Kapil Dev.

Coming back to the boys and cricket at TAFS. It is hard to say but I was the opening fast bowler of the class cricket team. It seems to me like a dream and I don't understand to this day how the great Vijay Arora and the fellow leader Amit Vij asked me to open the innings of the fielding side as a fast bowler. And I did not disappoint them at all. I did not take less than two wickets in the first over with my lethal yorkers. Nobody had an answer to my perfect yorkers and the leaders were very happy with me, always. Life is strange indeed and I have no regrets of never playing professional cricket in my life.

Seasons came and went and slowly we were taken to the arts class. This was a huge hall and the very first glimpse of the canvasses, paintings, rubber stencils, rollers, paint brushes with colored tips, sculptures, etc., thrilled me and I just wanted to try my hand at each of them. The duration of the class, I felt, was not enough. When I began to look at the various tools and implements to the point of digging in and contemplate my own masterpiece, the bell would ring and we had to leave at once, because other students were waiting outside. Here I must mention two names

– Himanshu Rai and Prabhdeep. Himanshu was good with rubber stencils and rollers and his impression on canvas with the help of stencils made me dumbfounded. I tried to do it myself, because I thought it was too exciting, but my small frame could not bring out a near perfect effect. Himanshu often said that his mother worked as a T.V. announcer at Doordarshan. I believed in everything that I was told, just like an innocent child, too naïve and gullible. Growing up I doubted the fact very much. Prabhdeep was a genius in the sixth grade. He was an excellent cartoon artist. I saw him drawing Phantom from the comic series to perfection from memory, not even looking at the figure while drawing. I have no idea what happened to him later in life but I understood one thing – there are certain people that are child prodigies and God perhaps hands them the tools and the passion too early in life so that they could lead a life of a successful artist. For the rest of the crowd, too common and ordinary, life may or may not happen and they could even die without knowing what they are good at.

Then came a soft manipulator called Amit Vatal without two of his front teeth. He suggested to me that life can be a breeze by manipulating a particular situation and especially people that seem to cause harm intentionally behind ones back. He was a smiling kid, not very tall but wiry. I walked with him during lunch breaks and would often end up in the makeshift canteen having hot samosas. He was never punished by the teachers because he had a way to save himself from difficult situations where a punishment was imminent. He had this quality of keeping his mouth shut when the teacher picked him up among the crowd and asked him if he was the one that had done a wrongful act of causing harm to a fellow student, etc. Without words he just could not be punished. And he had all the bullies of the class on his side and no one could utter a word without their permission. If there was the case of an unfinished homework, he handed his copy to the studious kid before the class and asked him to replicate the homework quickly. Usually, the studious kind was always like a bird in cage and did not ask any questions. And he had a way to get all those kids that were a bit peeved with him to the makeshift canteen for two hot samosas. Had he given the same treatment to me, I cannot tell. Yet he was a darling with his toothless smile and a free-spirited attitude, and I loved him. I have no idea where he is right now. When it came to me, I never failed to open my mouth and admit my failure to complete my homework, but I never did pester anyone, especially the bullies and the master of all bullies, Amit Vatal. I was asked quite often to stand outside the class for the whole period as punishment.

Such was the heap of talented boys and girls and The Air Force School, Subroto Park, New Delhi. There is however a paradox and I have never understood why. I have never heard the names of any of the above talented children. I do not know what happened to the boys and a handful girls later in life. None of them were ever heard on the national stage or higher. That year was 1985 when I was a student at TAFS. About forty years have gone by. I have lost both my parents. It was about twelve years ago, when I was thirty-seven that I developed interest in writing and reading. I have carried that interest since then and have made some strides towards being a published author.

For some people it all happens to early. But history has shown that those who start early, burn out too soon. There comes a time when there is a dearth of creativity in them, as of the lemon being totally squeezed out of its juices. For creativity and art need sacrifice to transcend to a higher state of mind. Knowing life and its mysteries is the most difficult thing in the world. People that feel safe in art after being baptized too early in it will not progress to a higher state of art and will be locked after amassing a certain level. Higher the sacrifice, higher the art.

I have had many friends and acquaintances starting from the time I was pushing towards youth. I traced the names of the stalwarts of the Air Force school and it presents a sorry picture. Those boys that had the shine of a million during that period were caught up in the rat race of life and did not pursue their artistic inclinations. Some that did, did not get too far.

Life demands sacrifice as in giving one's life to serve others, like parents, etc. True love is when we part with our love for good. And if it comes back then we ought to take it further.

Art is a product of human imagination and the greater the height, the greater the imagination leading to a greater perfection.

# CHAPTER ELEVEN

# THAT AMBITIOUS UNCLE

## TRUE AMBITION

Alexander the Great wanted to conquer the world, and he did, only later to give up the entire idea, as rather 'absurd'? Ashoka the Great killed a million as if he loved the colour red, only later to realize the futility of his efforts and became a Buddhist monk. It is said that foreign conquerors henceforth just gave him a smile and took away anything they wanted. Why does ambition always turn out that way when the thing conquered does not bring a lasting peace of mind and a realization of having reached the end of desire.

My great uncle was not an offshoot off the book of Alexander or Ashoka. Yet this man was very ambitious. The only ambition in any young man or woman till today, especially in the north and east part of this country is to become an IAS officer by cracking the UPSC exam. It is said that this exam is the toughest in the world and on successfully cracking it brings a lasting transformation in the individual. The person becomes a lover of books, a worldly person by knowing exactly what is happening in this world, has his own voice, carrying weight in his ideas making him a participant in a world not meant for commoners and invariably he or she now carries a heavy load on the nose bridge. But as they say, UPSC is not for the casual approach or someone that flaunts being as aspirant or for someone who is not prepared to read the last word in every book ever written in this world. It is just not an easy thing to do and many times there are aspirants who sit at the exam for six to seven years and still don't make it, and many do, showing how tough and gritty they really are. Failures are hard to chew and a person that has seen only success so far, can be at the least be extremely disappointed.

This uncle of mine, Mr. Brajesh Sinha, was known for his success at cracking any exam. At school he never stood second in class, always third from the top. Once he decided to break the jinx and got sick from studying late into the night when others were fast asleep. The next morning, he had a fever and his parents gave him two strong dozes of paracetamol in the morning with his milk. At the exam hall he thought he knew everything but somehow his brain was not responding by supplying him what he knew. As a result, he did not do well in the exam, although he knew everything. The result was a sickening fifth rank in the class and he is said to have hung his head in shame before the boys that just wanted to needle the genius with an unusual drop of two spots. He did not eat anything for two whole days but on the third day he gouged himself with jalebis, samosas and all the trash at the sweet shop. There was an undisclosed trick which my uncle had perfected at school that even his parents were unaware of. He understood the fact that it did not matter how much went into his head at the end of the day, all that mattered was the exam. And he just sat in his room trying to guess the exam questions and their answers. The biggest trick he employed was sitting with boys that always stood first in class, borrowing their notes, and making them friends for life. It then did not matter if he did not attend school for a couple of days and walked to the cinema hall for the latest Dilip Kumar film, instead, without the knowledge of his parents. The honest road is not meant for everyone. It is very long, slow and there's no surety of success even after that. My uncle even copied the idiosyncrasies of the brilliant students, he sat the way they did, laughed the way they did and swung the pen on his fingers just like them. Success is a big fat book. People like my uncle did not have the time to read every page and let patience settle matters for good. Instead, he turned the page to the exercises, worked out problems and set up a model paper of the coming exam in his mind beforehand. To make success a certainty he chuckled before boys that seemed to defy their age, and could spin a line on their lips by reading it just once from the book. Their mind was sharp with a retention power next to none.

That is the story of my uncle and how he passed every exam with flying colours to reach a point of flight by appearing at his first UPSC exam. My uncle left his home, his job, to come to stay with us in New Delhi and prepare for the UPSC exam. Home was too comforting and the job just knew how to make a person go crazy with unfinished files and deadlines sucking the life out of him. My father was an Air Force officer serving the HQ of the Western Air Command at Subroto Park, New Delhi. My brother and me were students of the Air Force School, Subroto Park, New Delhi. My mother was a homemaker and made sure there was food on the table three times a day among other things. She got excited to hear that her younger brother, Brajesh, was coming to their place looking for a place to prepare for the UPSC exam. He was to share the room with the boys and prepare for the exam in total silence and seclusion. My uncle was the first person in the family to move in the direction of Civil Services and try and capture a high rank at the UPSC exam.

He arrived one Saturday when the entire family was at home. He wore a brown leather jacket, fancy cotton trousers, huge black shoes, a wrist watch, a huge bag carrying his belongings, small bag on the shoulders for access to things used very often, and above all a bottle green Rayban goggles that made him look like a film star. His hands were buried deep into his jacket pockets when we saw him at the door with curious eyes. A slight bend of the shoulders like trying to touch the feet of my father and mother, followed by our lunge forward to touch his feet. He walked in with a smile and soft mumble lending him an air of grace. We pulled a chair for him at the dining table where my mother was ready with hot tea in a huge pot that was a part of an elegant tea set. There was the delicacy of Darbhanga and perhaps the whole of Bihar, which is our home, samosa and kachori and some slices of English tea cakes that had resins in them. My uncle did not touch the samosa, as a part of his continuing grace and hardly said anything, acting like a newlywed bride.

"So, young man, you want to be an IAS, that is a noble thought. We have a small separate room prepared for you in case you want to study the entire night. I wish you the very best and please try the samosa, I just brought it from Shalimar, the best sweet shop in the area."

My father did not say much about what he thought about the exam or offer tips on how my uncle could prepare better. And my father had a great insight into these exams, although he never ever gave one.

Very soon my uncle got down to a white pyjama and a white vest. On a usual day one could find him running through his handwritten notes and twisting his toe finger while lying on the bed cross legged. He had a fixed routine and very soon he roped in the little boys into his schedule. He woke us up at five in the morning and were pushed out of our beds. We reluctantly got up and went to the adjoining field for morning exercise. He made us run around the paved field that was very huge. He asked us to run by holding our breath just like he did. He said that it could enhance the bodily functions and strength. I could never run without my breath and did not care what my uncle said. We ran four to five rounds until we stopped to calm the racing heart beat while he kept running, perhaps to show how manly he was. We got back home and prepared for school while our uncle suddenly disappeared from our sight. While waiting at the bus stop for the bus we saw our uncle hiding something in his fingers. When we saw smoke coming out of his nostrils and mouth, we understood what he was up to. But he didn't want us to know and so he smoked secretly.

My uncle had a good life with us, so he said. He didn't have to wash his clothes, pay rent, cook food, or worry about returning home on time. He would step out when he liked and came home to eat when hungry. My mother would not mind feeding him even at odd hours. We never ever felt that he was living with us. My father was too busy with his job, hurting at the exploits of the Western Air Command. He wanted to quit and look at the wonderful stones handed to him by God, through his wife. His greatest wish in life was to convert these stones into diamonds by hammering and beating them to the extent of melting them in fire. He never ever disclosed this secret to anyone, not even his wife. He did not know why he held such a desire for two boys that were beyond foolishness.

My father just smiled when he saw my uncle and asked,

"Dear old chap, how is your preparation coming along? If you need any kind of help or assistance, please let me know. I hope these boys are not bothering you. If so, please let me know, I know how to set them right. Take care, young man."

My father wished my uncle well with all his heart. He really wanted the young man to succeed. But he did not know why he thought that there was something missing in my uncle's preparation. If he knew at all, he would have passed it on to my uncle, even if my uncle felt bad. My uncle was not a man digging into lengthy articles in the newspapers, reading all in the magazine called 'Career and Competition', or pushing his eyes reading novels. I have no idea what he read and how he prepared. But as habit would dictate, he must have sat all day trying to figure out the questions in the prelims. My mother often said that his brother worked very hard and did not go after those birds of desire that a young man usually does. Instead, he locked himself inside the small room and did not come out at all. Yet he could not resist the holler for a cup of hot tea early in the morning and late into the night when he was about to start his all-night freeze into the world of books.

I have often looked at this man through all the years and wondered what I did not do or try to do in my entire life. Did someone ask me what I wanted to be when I grew up, when I was all of eight. I'm sure this young man at my age would have had a bunch of answers, all showing his excitement and passion early in life. Yes, he wanted to be this and that with a hidden desire to walk the road of the greatest man that ever stepped on this earth- maybe like the great Alexander, or king Ashoka. It is not bad to have ambitions, in fact it is the source of motivation for any person on this earth and a man without one is no man at all. Yet my life taught me that the greatest ambition that I might have had was to remove the shades perpetual sadness in the eyes of my father. As a child I looked at my parents very carefully. I saw my father continuously struggling to make ends meet and my mother just too caught up in her house work. They struggled in a small home with meagre means. Very often they fought with one another like wild beasts and I was caught in a motionless state of mind, crying in total ignorance. To this day I have not forgot my tears, too late for my parents have left me.

Those days with my uncle passed too quickly. I did not get to talk to him much, maybe because I was an eleven-year-old child that does not have much to say.

Pretty soon my uncle disappeared and I did not see him at all after that. My Nana and Nani, parents of my uncle were not allowed to speak when my uncle sat with them and narrated tales of his success and how he cleared all his exams in engineering college with flying colours. My Nani just smiled and blessed her son.

Many years later I came to know that my uncle could not clear the prelims of the UPSC exam. He then appeared at IES exam (Indian Engineering Services) and cleared it to swat a government job. It is said that my vocal uncle did not show his face to his parents for over a year. And when he did, my Nani was in tears and was so happy that her son had landed a government job. She threw a party on the success of my uncle and seriously thought of the next step, lest my uncle had his own set of birdies on the sly. Anyhow my Nani never wanted to hear about them and did not care what my uncle wished. She began the search for a nice family girl of a reputed family, in the same caste.

Time passed too quickly. I grew from an eleven-year-old to a fifty-year-old male. My uncle manipulated his way through life and made sure his pockets were full at all times, by fair and unfair means. He did not go far, certainly not an Alexander or Ashoka. Great ambitions require great sacrifices. To feel for someone and to give one's life for others is the greatest virtue that will ever be in a world where no one is prepared to do anything for anyone. Gone are the days when humanity was the greatest ambition. It did not matter what happened to the individual, he or she did what they were told and followed the word of truth that comes from the soul and that is the hardest to follow.

*'Hear someone speaking every time,*
*you hear someone cry,*
*That cry calls for a shoulder,*
*And we must in all humanity,*
*Lend a helping hand,*
*Lest tears dry up too soon.'*

www.ingramcontent.com/pod-product-compliance
Lightning Source LLC
Chambersburg PA
CBHW040818120726
48005CB00012B/1454